challenging the
PACIFIC

Also by Maud Fontenoy

Across the Savage Sea:
The First Woman to Row Across the North Atlantic

challenging the
PACIFIC

THE FIRST WOMAN
TO ROW THE KON-TIKI ROUTE

MAUD FONTENOY

Translated from the French by Anthony Roberts

Arcade Publishing
New York

Arcade Publishing books may be purchased in bulk at special discounts for sales promotion, corporate gifts, fund-raising, or educational purposes. Special editions can also be created to specifications. For details, contact the Special Sales Department, Arcade Publishing, 307 West 36th Street, 11th Floor, New York, NY 10018 or arcade@skyhorsepublishing.com.

Arcade Publishing® is a registered trademark of Skyhorse Publishing, Inc.®, a Delaware corporation.

First published in France as *Le Pacifique a mains nues* by Editions Robert Laffont

Visit our website at www.arcadepub.com.

10 9 8 7 6 5 4 3 2 1

Library of Congress Cataloging-in-Publication Data is available on file.

ISBN: 978-1-61145-504-5

Printed in the United States of America

To Chris, guardian of my dreams

You see things, and you say, "Why?"
But I dream things that never were,
and I say, "Why not?"

—George Bernard Shaw

Contents

challenging the
PACIFIC

THE ROUTE

Departure from Lima, Peru, on January 12, 2005
Arrival at Hiva Oa, French Polynesia, on March 26, 2005

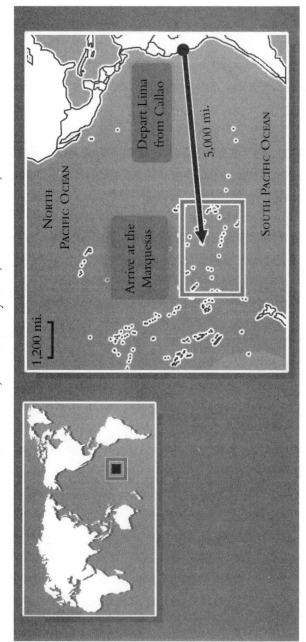

1

Emergency Dive

*T*HE SHARK CAME IN WITHOUT A SOUND, coldly slicing through the ocean. I fought to stay calm. *Whatever you do, stay where you are. Stay quite still in your seat.*

My eyes were fixed on the sleek, tapering shape just beneath the surface beside me. I was frozen with fright, my pulse racing, my insides tense and burning. All that lay between me and this dark blue menace was a film of water. With its cold eyes and steely musculature, the creature seemed invulnerable. It veered lazily around *Océor,* my cockleshell rowboat, like a lone wolf looking for prey. *Océor'*s sides shuddered with the vibration of its movement.

This one was probably cruising for sea bream, which were plentiful in the vicinity — and delicious, as I could attest. It was well over six feet long, and despite my panic I quietly thanked my stars I'd stuck to my strict resolution never to go swimming off the boat. Terrified and breathless, feeling very small indeed in the presence of this sleek predator, I could only sit and pray it would lose interest and go hunting elsewhere.

And suddenly it was gone, for no apparent reason. Maybe it thought I was too large a morsel.

This surprise visit occurred several days ago, around noon. I had just stopped rowing and was finishing off a ration of freeze-dried spaghetti Bolognese, dreaming of the beautiful fresh salads I hadn't seen for weeks. The shark's sudden appearance had made me drop the small aluminum-foil package containing my meal — and for some time after the thought of that great sinister shape made the hair rise on the back of my head. This was my first close shark encounter of the voyage. Nor was it the last, by any means.

Little did I know that within days I'd be agonizing about whether to break my resolution.

Should I or shouldn't I go over the side?

Under my feet, sixteen thousand feet of void stood between me and the ocean floor. I was more than twenty-five hundred miles from my port of departure, Lima, Peru. Alone in a vast expanse of sea, I had long since lost any physical sense of where I was. I was marooned in the presence of the elements. I couldn't afford the smallest error of judgment: there wasn't a soul to help if I ran into trouble.

The memory of all the blue-skinned sharks I had sometimes glimpsed swimming stubbornly around my boat filled me with dread. My brain churned with conflicting thoughts. *I mustn't make a wrong move.* Weak in the knees, I told myself stories to bolster my courage and relieve my sense of being so utterly alone.

Should I or shouldn't I?

The question kept resonating, like a bell tinkling to the rhythm of my body. My oar strokes had grown more and more leaden, ineffectual, painful. Seaweed had crept into the cockpit, which hadn't drained properly since the hawse pipes got choked by shellfish a while back. Recently, a stealthy growth of sea organisms had made its appearance beneath my sliding seat, making the tiny living space as slippery as soap. A few days earlier, the rudder had finally jammed, befouled by shellfish, and now it wouldn't shift to port. Worst of all, *Océor*'s hull, completely covered by hundreds of barnacles, was virtually dead in the water.

For several more days I hesitated. Torn between the fear of diving beneath the surface and the ever more pressing need to do something, I nevertheless battled on with the oars. The situation grew more critical by the hour. I knew if I waited much longer the boat would come to a complete standstill. I had to make a decision.

The sea was in an untidy, ruffled mood and we were riding a slow swell from the southward. But *Océor* wasn't herself. Instead of scudding over the waves, she was plunging heavily, like a wounded animal. The sky began to darken, and before long the ocean began to boil like a giant witch's cauldron. My tiny craft was also my lifeboat — I had nothing else. I gripped the oars like a couple of panhandles to avoid pitching sideways.

So, the idea of going overboard in this. . . .

I shut my eyes, trying to picture myself lying beside a huge pool, swimming peacefully, letting the fresh water run softly along my flanks, relishing the bliss of relaxation. My family would be near me. Anya, my two-year-old niece, would run over to me, wanting to be caught up in my arms . . .

Océor heeled dully to port, jolting me back to reality. It wouldn't be easy going over the side. I was bound to have trouble hauling myself back into the cockpit. The boat's hull was heavily rounded, which made her roll crazily at the best of times. I might even capsize her with the weight of my body.

But the moment came when I couldn't procrastinate any longer. I had no option. I had to careen *Océor,* or stay here forever.

I had run into this same situation before, when I rowed across the North Atlantic. It had been early October, and the water temperature was no more than 57 degrees Fahrenheit. I was paralyzed by fear and cold — I'll never forget the anguish of finding myself physically incapable of climbing back on board. I'd spent more than forty-five minutes in the water and couldn't summon the strength to hoist myself back up.

That ugly episode had taught me a valuable lesson,

and now, minutes away from an equally perilous venture, I felt helpless, vulnerable, and more terrified than ever. Because this time my body, my mind, and every other part of me knew exactly what to expect.

I had the morbid sensation that I was dipping too deeply into my reserve of luck. I felt under scrutiny, as if some imaginary being somewhere up above was waiting patiently for me to jump. I got a certain consolation in reminding myself that I always reflected carefully before making any move — and I had done so in this case. Maybe that would be a point in my favor.

I tend to deal with fear in the most Cartesian way possible, a little trick that has helped me overcome more than a few obstacles and difficulties. I divide the mountains I have to climb into small segments, which makes them somehow more accessible and less frightening. Of course, that's not the whole answer. Often the summit stays firmly hidden in the clouds, the path is steep and rugged, fatigue overwhelms me, and I long for only one thing: to stop, stop everything, now.

But then you learn patience and, because it is the only way, wait for the storm to abate and the right moment to come.

I knew I had to do this, even though my rational mind urged me to stay quietly in the cockpit. We all have an instinct to protect, even overprotect, ourselves. People sometimes ask what gives me the strength to get up and go when others prefer to stay put. Well, maybe I've worked out how to cut the current of reason, how to trip the circuit breaker and take a step into that so often paralyzing unknown.

Anyway, I made up my mind. I reached for the precious satellite phone, switched it on, and called planet Earth.

"Maman?"

"Darling, what's happening? It's only seven P.M. here. Why are you calling so early? Are you in trouble?"

"No, everything's fine. I just wanted to let you know — as I promised — that I'm getting ready to go over the side and scrape *Océor*'s bottom. I'm not happy about it, but the problem's really out of hand. *I absolutely have to.*"

"Well, if you must, you must. But please be careful. . . . And stay in touch. Call me when you're safely back on board. Promise?"

"Don't worry, I'll be fine, speak to you in a while. Big hug!"

"And keep a lookout for sharks!"

Then I perched on the edge of the cockpit, the soles of my feet slapped by the water each time *Océor* rolled. I clung on tightly, waiting for the right moment so that I wouldn't suddenly fall. This first dive into the vast Pacific, over whose surface I'd been drifting for upward of two months, didn't amuse me one bit. But now my mask was clamped on my face. I was harnessed, tied to the boat by a lifeline, and ready to go.

Who believes in guardian angels?

My mind flew back to the last few days of backbreaking effort with the oars, and the memory gave me a surge of courage. It was time to take action.

The moment came, and I jumped.

The water, a warmish 74 degrees Fahrenheit, still seemed chilly to me. I opened my eyes and beheld an immense shoal of black-and-white-striped pilot fish, all different sizes, waiting to greet me. They seemed quite unafraid. Although it was a scene of troubling beauty, I wasn't disposed to dwell on it. Lower down, hovering above a monstrous black void that made me pull my legs hurriedly to the surface, were scores of bonitos. They observed me with fishy detachment.

The light was dim. I felt like some jiggling live bait impaled on a hook.

I didn't dare try to imagine what might be lurking in that yawning inky abyss. My legs were kicking at full speed, as if afraid of being sucked into those miles of emptiness below. Without so much as another look into this underwater abyss, I set about scraping off the thick layer of crustaceans attached to the hull. My sole objective was to get it clean and spend as short a time as possible in the water.

I had a long, very sharp knife, and I used it to slash at the bases of the barnacles. These small, cream-colored shellfish, ribbed with orange, whose suckers can cling to the most effective anti-fouling varnish, began to fall away in a swirl, as if drawn downward by a giant siphon. To see them vanishing so quickly into nothingness made my flesh crawl. I forced myself to look up and attend to the task at hand. The rudder was completely sheathed in barnacles — no wonder it was jammed!

Working quickly, I freed it up, as I kept looking around, checking to make sure that my sense of a hostile presence was only an eerie illusion. Visibility was no more than a few feet, and I was well aware I'd have no time to scramble out of the water if a shark should happen by. When I came to the surface for air, my feet were tingling with terror. The waves kept pulling me away from *Océor;* each time a wave hit it was more of a struggle to get back alongside. Meanwhile, swarms of pilot fish darted around my hands, snapping at barnacle flesh as I ripped it off the hull. The smallest ones, completely fearless, came right up to my mask and banged up against the glass.

I had a sudden flashback. . . .

I was a child, swimming off my family's schooner where she lay at anchor in some heavenly Caribbean bay. The crafty little fish crowded up so close I was sure they'd get in my ears. But my two brothers were nearby, and I was also reassured by the broad, fat bottom of our boat, which looked from a distance like the belly of a whale.

Today's excursion with the pilot fish, however, was altogether different, and a strange presentiment jerked me violently back into the present. Before my eyes, in a split second, every one of my swimming companions vanished into the murky depths. I was suddenly all alone, breathless, my stomach in knots, my legs drawn up to my chest, barely able to move. All sorts of scenarios flashed through my mind. The disappearing act was a hideous alarm. The danger was very near. Without losing a moment, staying as calm as I could, I struck out for the side of the boat.

I needed to get out of the water — on the double!

But *Océor* was wallowing so badly I couldn't do it. Clinging with all my strength to the guard rail, I tried to catch hold of something in the cockpit, but my fingers slipped. Again *Océor* pitched sideways. Without warning, a wave hit me hard and I went under. I felt as if I were drowning. Morbid images flooded through my head. I was furious at myself for getting into this grotesque mess.

Come on, Maud, said a weary inner voice. *You did it in the Atlantic. You can do it here, too.*

Deliberately using my legs as little as possible, I concentrated hard, channeling every ounce of energy into my arms. At that moment I'd have done anything to get back aboard. At which point a convulsive heave combined with a sudden roll of the boat sent me tumbling into the cockpit, where I impaled myself on a stainless steel thwart. I let out a yelp of pain.

My rib. Cracked again, in the same place as before, when I banged it during a terrible storm in the Atlantic. This was all I needed.

With one hand clamped to the wound, I struggled to hold back my tears. I'd been unforgivably clumsy. Now I wanted to avenge my sore body, which I knew would hurt till the day I ended the voyage. A cracked rib plagues you mercilessly, hour after hour, until you give in and stop moving. It was going to be like that from now on. I was drained and shaking with pain, but I couldn't hide behind that for very long. I had to go back in the water — the other side of the hull also needed to be scraped. I wished myself far away from this ocean and its endless, relentless pressures.

Come on, Maud, back in the saddle with you!

The voice of my riding instructor, Jean-Paul B., welled up in my memory. Never let too much time elapse between the time you fall off (and God knows I fell off a lot) and the time you remount. Gritting my teeth so as not to let on I'd hurt myself, I vowed to silently do as I was told and clamber back on the horse.

Here in the Pacific, instead of dusting off my pants I rubbed my hair with a towel, caught my breath, and made a conscious effort to empty myself of trepidation.

The sea ground its teeth. The waves raked along *Océor*'s sides with deliberate menace. Feverishly, I looked around for sharks' fins breaking the surface, but saw none among the pelting crests and troughs. I prayed the danger was past, whatever it had been, and peered overboard, hoping to see my shoal of pilot fish back in place. Finally, taking a deep breath, I reluctantly slithered over the starboard side to finish the job I'd begun.

I love the water, but I'd never been so unhappy about going into it as I was at that moment.

The ocean was empty of fish, but I was still tempting fate. The weather was growing more threatening by the minute, and soon the seas would be too high for me to have a chance, however hard I tried, of getting back on board. Gripping my big diving knife, I did the careening as quickly as I could, breaking the surface every minute or so to breathe.

The sun was hidden now, and I could see almost nothing. Remoras, little black sucking fish, were tightly wedged around the desalinator tube; I scraped them off before they could do any more damage. Buffeted against the hull to which I was attached, I swallowed mouthfuls of seawater. But I stuck to the job, and after thirty horrible minutes it was done. I heaved myself up hand over fist on the mooring line. It was an exhausting maneuver, even more difficult than the first time, and by the time I reached the cockpit I was aching all over, as weak as a kitten.

But I was proud of what I had done. Indeed, I was happy, too, relieved to have completed the job. I quietly gave thanks to the Great Universe for protecting me from real harm. Superstitious as I am, I was sure that my "resolutely disciplined" side had not gone unappreciated somewhere.

Sore, solitary, and exhausted — but safe.

I sat there and began to laugh.

2

A New Challenge

MY WINDOW AT THE AGENCY faced a pizzeria, where ten red motorbikes were drawn up, each with a little delivery box perched on the passenger seat. Since I often worked late, I occasionally would watch the machines humming to and fro like bees around a hive, responding busily as the orders came in. Between errands, the delivery men milled around the pizzeria door and smoked cigarettes to pass the time in the frozen December weather. Huddled in identical red jackets embossed with their employer's logo, they waited with patient resignation for the next call to come through. Then, around midnight, activity ceased and the bikes were carefully chained together. Free at last, the men in red hurried away to their homes. But there was no escape for their machines — they'd be parked on the pavement till next evening.

Sitting on my plush swivel chair, I felt as chained to my own destiny as those silent motorbikes ranked in their slots across the street. A pile of fat files sat on the desk be-fore me. I worked as a building manager and I loved the job, to which I brought the same passion as to everything else I did. I especially liked the on-site meetings I attended with architects; often the builders would see me turn up in a suit and high heels and politely suggest I wait below, at ground level. Their concern made me smile — I was used to swarming up scaffold ladders four rungs at a time. Once I was aloft and looking out across the roofs of Paris, my mind would often wander away from whatever the site manager was saying, daydreaming of other wide open spaces. The countless houses and buildings of every size stretching away below reminded me of the crests and troughs of ocean waves; the urban limits to my field of vi-sion were like the sea's horizon.

I longed to see what lay beyond that horizon. I longed for the sea, adventure, the unknown. Every moment of my daily life they called to me. The Paris metro became a sub-marine in the depths of the ocean; the pigeons nodding on the agency's porch were seagulls blown from the open sea; the rain was an invigorating squall; even the drafts in my office carried a salt tang and clamored for me to board my tiny rowboat in time to catch the tide. As if that wasn't enough, I was surrounded by small reminders: the latest is-sue of *Voiles et voiliers* lay provocatively on a shelf, and pho-tos of *Pen Duick* and *Géant II Velsheda* majestically faced each other from opposite walls. On my closed door was an old sea chart of the Azores, which I had set aside along

with all the others I had used to set my Atlantic course —
my eyes kept returning to it, answering its unspoken sum-
mons. By the telephone, little jars of seawater, sand, and
broken shells beckoned. I had brought these home after a
regatta between the Granville and Chausey islands, and every
time I looked at them I'd be swamped with memories.

There were about fifteen of us in that race, and we
were determined to row the whole way. Our oar blades
weren't exactly ideal, and for my friends, most of whom
were armchair sailors or even landlubbers who'd never been
to sea, the going was rough. Plenty of crabs were caught in
the choppy water, and we were lucky not to get into worse
trouble. The boat I was on, the *Action,* built at Meaux, was
instrumental in converting me to rowing. The closeness to
the ocean, the calm, and the effort rowing required gave me
immense pleasure. Every one of those sea escapades, every
day stolen from my life as a building manager, reawakened
a painful longing for the water, for a new voyage.

Day and night, memories mingled chaotically of my
Atlantic crossing in 2003. I relived the fabulous sunsets, the
ecstasy of being at sea, the friendly encounters with whales,
as well as the icy nightmares of stormy weather, headwinds,
and leaden solitude. I remembered everything, and yet the
bad things gradually dissipated, giving way to fresh dreams. I
gave in to a burning desire to do, to build, to attempt again
what people had at the time dismissed — quite unfairly — as
folly. My head was full of plans; my excitement slowly rose
like the mercury in a thermometer, a wonderful sensation.

I was filled with new energy. My legs began to tingle; my whole body hummed. Like soup in a saucepan on the stove, I was going from a simmer to a boil, then over-flowing.

The moment came, as it always does, and I made my decision. I was going to row solo across the Pacific.

The idea had first occurred to me in the middle of the Atlantic. Obviously not during the big storm, when I capsized seventeen times in a single night, but very probably during the weeks that followed when things were going better and I was nearing the finish. During the storm, the prospect of starting over was too much to contemplate. To tempt fate with any more bad luck at sea was the last thing I wanted.

When I was back on land, the weeks went by with the speed of albatrosses slashing through the air to scoop their prey from the surface of the sea. I was caught up in a rush of events linked to my Atlantic crossing. I could feel myself losing control of the situation, carried along by habit. I saw my little boat, miserably out of place beside the sluggish Marne, slowly subsiding into a corner of the garden. A distressing sight, she was high and dry between a horse chestnut tree and a pine, and it moved me to hatch a plan to set her free. In my mind I already saw her afloat again, the waves lapping against her, cradled and solaced by the breathing ocean.

Faced with the unavoidable, I allowed myself to reconsider the idea. Crossing the Pacific would be the logical next step: to enter regions that were virtually deserted, to open up a new frontier for the sport of rowing, to prove a second time that such exploits were much less a matter of strong arms than of willpower and determination. The desire to go out and tackle the giant was burning inside me. *I would take on the mighty Pacific,* the mythical ocean that had nourished my dreams when as a child I first read the great sea stories of exploration, discovery, and whale hunting. I have always had, so to speak, an open porthole in my heart, which looks out on the main and makes me yearn for something more, something different.

By the month of February, when I officially informed my family and friends of my intention, the project had already been ripening in my head for several months. I was only waiting for the right moment to announce it. I was aware that my mother would have preferred news of a pregnancy or a forthcoming marriage, and I knew only too well that it wouldn't be easy to convince her that this new expedition was a good idea. Nevertheless, my family supported me to the hilt, as always. We are a close-knit tribe, ready to fight tooth and nail for our kinfolk.

Our family boat, which I boarded for the first time when I was barely a week old, was my home for fifteen years thereafter. I grew up in an atmosphere of fierce solidarity that, along with an unconventional education, has helped immensely in bringing my projects to fruition. My brothers and I were responsible for ourselves at a very early age. We settled on our own punishments; we had the right to do as we pleased; and as a result we always tried to do the best we could. Our sense of looking out for ourselves and each other kept us in check more effectively than our parents could have (though Marc and Chantal always kept an eye on us). Practically from babyhood, we habitually did things on our own. Whether swimming around the boat or taking the dinghy ashore to fetch bread in the mornings, stowing a sail or standing by with a radio receiver, we learned to be watchful and disciplined. And these qualities proved immensely helpful to me later on my solo voyages, when I had no margin for error.

My mother remembers that when I was a little girl and had some detailed job to do, if someone tried to help I would push them away, repeating over and over, "Me do, me do!" So my preference for getting things done under my own steam is no recent phenomenon.

Now I was going to head off again on a new adventure, stripped down to its purest, simplest essentials. This is the way I like to work. My boat would not be fitted out with any complicated electronic gadgets, computer, automatic pilot, or router. I would embark on a tiny boat made of red cedar strip planking, her hull one-third of an inch thick, covered in fiberglass to make it hermetic. My little *Océor* would doubtless have been lighter had she been made of carbon fiber, but she also would have been a great deal more expensive, and I didn't have the money.

The Pacific challenge needed plenty of careful preparation. First my plan had to be ripened, rounded, made digestible and acceptable. If you want credibility, you need to demonstrate solid motivation, show that you've thought things through. Problems have to be simplified, gray areas illuminated. I'd learned in the past, little by little, to take into account all the risks and reckon with every possible danger or difficulty, and have solutions ready before my departure.

The first thing to decide was exactly when I could leave. I studied the pilot charts, which indicate winds, currents, and storm probabilities, and concluded on the basis of that information that I should embark at the beginning of the year. I prepared to spend a summer in the Southern Hemisphere, calculating that I would reach the first Polynesian islands after the cyclone period. Having settled on these dates, I needed to put together a team, find sponsors, modify my boat, organize my departure, put together my equipment, get a medical checkup, and work through the weather reports — not to mention visit children in the schools and hospitals that might sponsor me, give talks and attend conferences to finance the initial expenses, and at the same time run, swim, and row when I got home in the evenings.

In short, I had more than enough to keep me occupied.

The search for sponsors was long, drawn out, and awkward, full of disappointments and frustrations. It was far from easy to sell a project as crazy as this one. Most of my letters were completely ignored or answered with form rejections. There were any number of sterile meetings and barren telephone calls.

You begin by not getting discouraged. Just feeling ready to see a project through to the finish isn't enough; you have to be lucky enough to communicate your enthusiasm. For me, that luck came through Jean-Francois Copé, who introduced me to Thierry Gaubert and then to Charles Milhaud, the president of the Caisses d'Epargne savings group. Little was said during our first interviews — it was a lot like taking an exam, being carefully evaluated from tip to toe.

I kept reminding myself, when I speak, stick to the bare essentials. Be as concise as possible. That way I was able to stay calm under the intense scrutiny.

Several months went by. I stayed on course, fought to reduce my budget by seeking out technical sponsors, and generally kept up the pressure. Finally, at the beginning of August, the answer came: Mr. Milhaud had decided to back me, and the Bank of Tahiti (a branch of Financière Océor) would be my principal sponsor. It was an extraordinary relief. Now I was all set.

I'd already picked up my co-sponsor after speaking at a seminar in Marrakech, on behalf of Burton, the ready-to-wear company. I got on well with their managing director, Claude Cosquer, and very soon I had an agreement in principle with the head of the Omnium Group, Robert Lascar, who allowed me to start believing that whatever happened now I was definitely going to the Pacific. I was, and still am, hugely grateful to him.

Then the City of Meaux, where I was born and which I still call home, offered to give me a major helping hand. Meaux quickly became my third sponsor and helped me form the backup team I needed to organize everything. Town Hall became the focal meeting point for schools, press, my family, and a large number of interested locals.

Michel Polacco, the head of the radio network France Info, also got involved, swinging the weight of that important party behind me. Christian Bex, who had covered my Atlantic crossing, was ready to be my press representative for the three months I would be at sea.

My boat, previously the *Pilot,* renamed *Océor,* was re-fitted at the Marine Technology yard at La Trinité-sur-Mer, where she was greatly improved. She was officially rechristened by the French TV broadcaster Patrick Poivre d'Arvor on November 15, 2004, in the gardens of the Ministère d'Outre-Mer in Paris, with Brigitte Girardin and Francois Lamour in attendance. So now I had serious and involved sponsors, a team, and a boat. The end of the year was fast approaching — time to pack.

I spent Christmas with my family. At the table, we were all reluctant to broach the subject of the Pacific; everyone pretended not to be thinking I'd soon be gone. I wondered if my mother was secretly praying for me to change my mind at the last minute. As for me, I tried my best to conceal my growing stress and concentrated on enjoying these last days in the company of the people I loved. I knew from experience how much I would miss such precious moments. I wanted to fill myself to bursting with everything that surrounded me: memories like this would help me combat the solitude of the ocean over the coming months.

I spent the evening of January 1 checking over my lists, trying to find room in my bags for everything I'd forgotten to put in the container with the boat. I had an agonizing bellyache, but kept it to myself. I rolled up the last ocean charts and stuffed them in a tube, packed my T-shirts in airtight plastic, recharged the batteries of the satellite telephone, picked out the few books I wanted to take, and sorted the documents I needed aboard. One corner of my bag was carefully set aside for the laminated family photos and children's drawings of flowers, countryside, and rich vegetation that would shortly decorate the interior of *Océor*'s cabin. Finally, I sealed away the letters that my guardian angel Chris — my boyfriend — my family, and my friends had written for me. Each one of them was worth its weight in gold. I would carry them in my hand luggage, to be sure they wouldn't be lost. Each one had instructions on the envelope such as: *Not to be opened till you're at sea. Read this as soon as you're clear of the Humbolt Current. For when you're halfway there. For the night before you land.*

Those letters were the most precious gifts I received that Christmas.

★   ★   ★

The heat was sticky and intense when I arrived in Lima, Peru's capital, with my dear friend Thomas, who helped me during the preparation of my boat, by my side. Founded by the conquistador Francisco de Pizarro in 1535, Lima is a great Pacific port. Yet it is also enveloped in a haze of pollution and is rampant with poverty, chaos, and ostentatious public buildings. What with the swarming population of seven million, hideous traffic congestion, and omnipresent heat, no wonder the air in the city is scarcely breathable.

As the plane banked toward the runway, I gazed humbly at the dirt-colored ocean along the coast. Scores of trawlers lined the quays like so many cockroaches, their derricks extended like insects' legs. Later contact with Lima did nothing to make me like it any better. And yet I had warm memories of Peru from my reconnaissance visit the previous August in the Andean town of Puno, on the banks of Lake Titicaca, the world's highest navigable lake, with an altitude of 12,556 feet.

Titicaca was the starting point of the legendary *Kon-Tiki* expedition across the Pacific made by Thor Heyerdahl and his friends. On the shores and islets of the lake are a sprinkling of ancient communities that have preserved their traditional ways of life. Myth has it that the first Inca, Manco Capac, emerged from the waters of Titicaca to found his empire on the orders of the Sun God. The mysterious

Uros tribe has lived on this enormous lake forever, on floating islands built with *totora,* a kind of reed that they also use to build their slender boats, which are propelled by oars or sails. Thor Heyerdahl, who fifty years ago took the same course across the Pacific that I now planned to follow, based his famous craft on these boats.

When I arrived in Lima I was happy, however, that at long last I would be rejoining my own little *Océor.* But it turned out to be a lot more difficult than I expected.

At noon on the following Friday morning — in other words more than a week after my arrival at the airport — Pascal, an expatriate working for the French embassy, and I laid siege to the offices of the transit agent. We had been waiting all that time for the customs officer to arrive, open the container, and officially admit my boat to Peruvian soil. But today, once again, it appeared that he was indisposed and we were wasting our time.

"Monday. Not before Monday," said the man behind the desk. He looked genuinely upset by his inability to help us. I implored him, trying to make him see that every day was vital to my preparations, and that the moment of my planned departure was fast approaching. He tried again. The fans creaked in his office, it was stiflingly hot, and the agent was drenched in sweat. Beside him, another eight people were working away silently. I paced up and down.

Finally, at the end of the long afternoon, having oscillated between *yes* and *no* at least eight times, the customs official agreed to leave and help us. We piled into the car and followed him down to the docks, where hundreds of containers were stacked. I was the only one allowed in. Somebody handed me a hard hat, and a little man in torn blue overalls told me to come with him. Anxiously, I watched as the steel box was opened, to reveal *Océor*'s nose peeking timidly into the light of day. I examined her; she seemed to be in one piece, to my great relief.

A dozen Peruvians dived into the box. Two of them went into the boat and routed out all my vacuum-packed property — T-shirts, underwear, powdered food. They went through every item, while I struggled to explain that the plastic bags couldn't be opened on any account. Everything had to stay hermetically sealed to keep the damp out. They looked at me, completely baffled. I couldn't make myself understood and I was terrified they would damage something.

Then one of the men, I think he was the youngest, discovered the posters stowed in a box in the cockpit. He slipped one into the official's hand: he grinned, told me I was pretty in the picture, then chuckled and gave me a squeeze. I realized everything was going to be okay.

Fifteen minutes later, the documents were signed and sealed and we were authorized to pick up the boat next morning. I'd been waiting for over a week, and according to my plans and my weather imperatives, I calculated I had only three days left to get everything ready.

Next morning, we were back in front of the agent's depot at 10:30 sharp. The blue container with *Océor* inside had been lifted onto a big truck. Fifteen figures were running around it like headless chickens. A minute later, the box was opened and six men scrambled in and started removing the ropes holding *Océor* in place. I started getting worried: decanting her safely was going to be awkward.

I rushed off to find the foreman to warn him that my boat was extremely fragile. We had to lower the container to the ground, move the animal gently out of her cage, find a trailer and a vehicle to tow her, hoist her onto the trailer, make everything fast, and then drive safely through the crazy Lima traffic to the Regata Club.

All this had to be done without crane, sling, or ramp. And as yet we had no trailer, either. I was seriously worried now — if *Océor* were damaged in even the slightest way, the whole trip was off. Tension mounted. I sorely missed my resourceful younger brother Roch in situations like this.

I took a deep breath. A half hour had passed. We looked calmly at the options, while the men sat around on the ground in whatever scraps of shade they could find. The heat was steadily becoming unbearable. Some of the men got up and fetched tools and materials in a desultory way, on the instructions of their boss. Their boss seemed ill at ease. I felt he hadn't quite grasped the urgency of the situation.

By noon, we'd managed to borrow a forklift and by one o'clock we had a second. The team set to work, the container rose into the air and I crossed my fingers till it was finally, delicately, deposited on the ground. We set about hauling the boat out by hand, and, as she emerged, the astonishment of the stevedores was evident. They stared at me, wide-eyed. For them, the most important thing was to earn enough to eat that day. My priorities as a representative of a wealthy Western society were totally different, and I was abashed.

But together we got on with the job, and within three-quarters of an hour my small craft was in the open air, wedged in place with motor tires that would probably adorn a car somewhere on the edge of town by nightfall. At two o'clock, the trailer kindly loaned to us by the rowing club was on the spot, and by three we had *Océor* loaded up, looking much too bulky for the trailer chassis. We lashed her in place as tightly as possible.

Five hours after the commencement of the operation, we arrived at the rowing club with our police escort. Given the time we had taken to get this far, and the state of the trailer (which was sagging quite seriously), I figured that if all we did was back *Océor* into the club's boathouse and leave her there overnight, it would take the better part of the following day to get her into the water. Moreover, I couldn't see how we'd ever be able to apply a final essential coat of anti-fouling varnish to protect the hull, what with all the tires and cordage festooning her. The yacht club was right next door, I reasoned; they had a crane for lowering boats into the water. I decided to go for it.

They told me there was no room, that I'd have to pay,

that in any case it was forbidden to paint boats on their premises. It was four o'clock; people were just finishing their lunches; in short, *go away.* But it was already the ninth of January, I planned to leave on the twelfth, and I still had a whole slew of things to install on the boat. I called my local guardian angel, Johnny, a Peruvian who was a major specialist in *pisco,* the local brandy, as well as fluent in English and French. He made a few calls for me, settled things in the local fashion, and by 4:30 *Océor* was hoisted up at the yacht club, ready to paint. At last! In short order, we had her rubbed down with sandpaper and set about coating her with anti-fouling varnish.

Passersby stopped to lend a hand or ask a question. People kept mentioning *Kon-Tiki* . . . and then asking where the person was who was going on this adventure. They had trouble believing it was me, with my long hair and my skinny arms. Even in France they didn't find it credible, but here people were so amazed they couldn't even grasp the fundamentals. It was simply inconceivable, out of the question, *impossible* that I should entertain the idea of rowing off alone across the Pacific. Looking back, I think many of them thought I was pulling their leg.

At 5:30, we began laying on the second coat — and half an hour later *Océor* entered, for the first time, the waters of the Pacific. It was a great relief to see her bobbing there; all the hard work was rewarded with this moment, and it made my heart soar. The sun was lower in the sky, the brutal heat had abated, and I felt good again. We lovingly towed *Océor* to a mooring buoy, which seemed safer than leaving her tied to the jetty. Everything was shipshape, and I went back ashore on a motorboat. Thomas and Pascal were on board another one, which broke down, so they had to row the rest of the way.

The entire next day was spent getting *Océor* ready for sea. Finding the buoy underwater at high tide, we moored her to a floating pontoon at the yacht club. Then I laid everything out on the platform to make an inventory. I needed to see every item clearly: food, clothing, navigation instruments, medical and hygienic supplies. For his part, Thomas focused on the electrical equipment.

Boats kept coming in nearby, and children wandered over to see what I was doing. The distraction made me worry about losing things in the water. The heat was stupefying — you couldn't spend more than a few minutes at a time in *Océor*'s cockpit, which was like a sauna.

The chairman of the yacht club dropped by to bid us welcome. Eager to help, the first thing he did was close the access to our work area so we could function in peace. He also told me that on the day I weighed anchor, he would gladly place his private motorboat at my disposal, a kindness that pleased me no end.

Marcel Mochet from the Agence France-Presse came to take some pictures. I don't think I was looking my best at the time — I was much too preoccupied — but I was careful to hide my face as well as I could under the brim of my hat. All of a sudden, I was thinking of the 4,500 miles of ocean that lay ahead of me; it sent shivers up my spine. Had I overestimated myself, my stamina, my courage?

The pile of supplies I was taking now seemed larger than the boat — how on earth would I ever manage to stow all of it in the tiny space available? I did a complete revision and laid in the strictest minimum. The Thermos cover would have to stay ashore, along with a few freeze-dried meals I felt were excessive, some T-shirts, storage boxes, and nonessential rolls of paper towels.

That evening we tested the water desalinator and found it in good working order. By 7 P.M., *Océor* was fully loaded and ready to go. It was cooler; I stretched out on my narrow pallet in the cabin and tried to get my bearings. Soon enough, I'd be heading for the open sea.

For a while I let myself be lulled by the low voices around me and the laughter of the Peruvian children playing in the water. Later, alone on the vast ocean, I would remember those sounds, imagine them close by, and feel better.

Tomorrow we would make the final tests of my equipment, after which all that remained was to hope for good weather. Luc Toullemans, my weatherman from Belgium, had sent the forecast for the next few days; the weather remained unclear. It looked likely, though, that I'd be leaving on schedule, on Wednesday, January 12, 2005.

I'd been spending the nights at an apartment shared by

Pascal, his wife, Elizabeth, and their son Robin, who had been living in Lima for three years. They looked after me, making sure I didn't bite my nails to the quick while I waited for my hour of deliverance. Even so, I felt very much alone, almost as isolated as I expected to be in a few days' time. I was anxious about the departure, which was bound to be complicated with uncertain weather prospects and two dangerous islands offshore from Lima. At the same time, I was pleased that I was about to end this land-based stage of the trip and excited to be setting off on a new adventure. Above all, I was impatient to be far, far away from this dangerous coast, though I knew I was likely to be pushed back on it by the elements, perhaps again and again.

Wednesday came at last. I had been preparing for this moment for a full year. It was four in the afternoon, and I was ready to loose my moorings and try to beat the heat by rowing throughout the night. I made a last call to my mother, sent a text message to Chris, then strode purposefully toward my shipmate, *Océor.* Peru's sports minister, Yvan Dibos, had turned up to wish me luck. We toasted each other with a *pisco* sour — I wasn't entirely sure this was a good idea, but I knew I'd be sick as a dog in a few hours whatever I drank. I was braced for three weeks of hell before I could extricate myself from the coast. The weather forecast indicated variable winds and currents that were bound to carry me northward no matter what I did, and I was bound to have trouble holding my course due west to Polynesia.

People started crowding onto the pontoon where *Océor* was moored. They scrutinized her from every angle; it seemed to me she puffed out her chest proudly. Several cameras were running as I fiddled with a few final details, like hanging fresh fruit in a net in the cabin. Then, after extracting my hairbrush from my sponge bag, I passed it ashore to Thomas. Only later did I realize that it contained my toothbrush.

A number of boats were waiting offshore to bid me farewell. It was time to set sail. A Peruvian navy vessel would be standing by for the first night to warn merchant vessels and container ships of my presence. One night was all they could spare, and it wasn't much. I wouldn't get very far in that short time, but it was something, and I was glad of their help. After that, I'd be spending about three weeks in a major shipping thoroughfare and fishing zone, and — according to the navy — well within reach of the pirates who cruised off the coast of Peru.

So there wasn't a moment to lose.

I pulled my oars from the forward hatch (I had three other pairs snugly stowed in the same place). My throat was tight with emotion. The mooring lines fore and aft were cast off, I gave the pontoon a shove with my foot, and positioned myself in my sliding seat. All the boats around me sounded their horns and sirens, the people waved, and the minister hailed *"Buen viaje, Maud!"* from his motor launch.

I grinned to hide my emotion.

I was off.

Océor had never felt so heavy; 1,300 pounds, to be exact, which I had to pull along with the sole strength of my arms. After a while, the last sailboat veered about and headed for shore. A few moments later, I said farewell to Thomas, Pascal, Elizabeth, and Robin. It was dusk; I switched on my nightlight, which blinked in time with my wildly beating heart. Then I gritted my teeth and rowed onward into the uncertain darkness.

The distant lights of the naval vessel were reassuring. I thought of the men aboard her, preparing dinner, keeping an eye on me watch by watch. With the first island of San Lorenzo astern, the swell increased markedly; this was my first encounter with the real Pacific. My eyelids drooped. The first hours of rowing were always painful, and I bitterly regretted my failure to train over the last days. And, just as I'd expected, I started getting seasick. Nearby a whale sounded and made me jump. I hoped it wouldn't come any closer. A container ship steamed past to starboard; I assumed she'd been warned of my presence. I longed for sleep, but another small island, Hormigas de Afuera, lay ahead and the current was dragging me toward it. Through the darkness, I could hear waves crashing on the rocks.

I raised the tempo of my rowing. It was the darkest hour of the night, my hands were already covered in blisters, my stomach was churning, and I was struggling to get out of danger. The navy ship was a long way off and it was unlikely her crew were aware of any problems I might have. I'd only been at sea for seven hours and already I felt vulnerable.

Dawn saw me still not clear of danger, rowing for my life to get past those evil, surface-level rocks of the island. It was the first morning of my voyage, and the navy vessel came alongside to say good-bye and Godspeed. The crew waved, and the helmsman gave three blasts of the foghorn. I interpreted that as my last chance to give up, abandon ship, and go home. I shuddered. But with a gentle roll *Océor* herself encouraged me to raise a determined hand and wave.

Satisfied that she'd carried out her mission, my escort sheered off and headed back to port. I watched her till she was no more than a black dot on the horizon. Then I bent to my oars. My hands were burning. Tears poured down my cheeks.

My course was set due west.

3

First Encounters

*F*ROM A DISTANCE, I could see their dark shapes swirling on the surface of the water. They would vanish for a moment, hidden behind a wave, then suddenly they'd be there again — swift, mysterious shadows, like nothing I'd ever seen before in the ocean. I dived into the cabin and resurfaced with the binoculars, which I always kept within reach. It was barely 9 A.M. and the sun was already beating down with a vengeance. I stood up straight, braced myself against the stern cowling, and focused in.

Five long black necks sprouted from the water. Sea lions!

Ever since my departure from the port of Callao, I had been rowing along the Humboldt Current, a mighty swath of cold water flowing northward toward the equator. It was a difficult zone to traverse. Ostensibly I was being swept to the north, and hence had to advance crabwise to make headway westward. Sea lions, unlike me, favored this part of the ocean because it offers the cool water they need to survive. Hunted nearly to extinction by the end of the nineteenth century, the species is now protected; the total population is currently thought to exceed forty thousand individuals.

Nowadays the main threat to sea lions is not hunting but climate change. In recent years El Niño has created a warmer surface current, which has raised the overall water temperature and wiped out large numbers of the squid and fish on which sea lions prey.

Sea lions were plentiful in the zone I was in, near the Galapagos. I'd already come across them on several occasions during the first two weeks of the voyage. This time, moving in small, playful groups, they drew closer, diving and resurfacing with apparent nonchalance. A camera swung at my neck. I sat motionless, waiting patiently for them to come alongside to examine my boat — and me — at close quarters. *Océor* fell almost tenderly silent, bobbing gently like a cork on the long, heavy swell, doing her best not to scare the visitors. The land was eons away; I was alone on a gigantic desert of salt water. This unexpected company gave me back my bearings, settled my soul, and I reveled in their presence. The ocean had generously revealed a tiny portion of the life within her, and in so doing had broken my gloomy sense of isolation.

I held my oars above the surface, to avoid making any stir in the water. Time stopped. I would wait for hours if need be, stock-still. I wasn't going to let this opportunity slip by. Compared with the months at sea that lay ahead, what did one or two extra hours matter? I needed these creatures like a draft of fresh water. Insignificant though they might seem by comparison with the 4,600 miles I had to cover, they filled a void inside me. Moments like this, stolen from the daily monotony of endless rowing, were among the most wonderful of a voyage I hoped to keep as simple and human as possible.

The sea lions were clearly inquisitive. They zigzagged discreetly in my direction. Now they were only thirty feet away, heads craning above the surface for a better view of me, as if astonished to encounter this strange creature. I didn't move a muscle, crouching in the cockpit to get a better view of them. Now the boldest ones, their dark skins glistening, were almost near enough to touch. Excited and enchanted, I willed myself invisible, desperately hoping they'd forget me.

Sea lions are a special kind of mammal, famous for their intelligence, their love of play, and their sonorous barking call. They were intrigued by *Océor* as she idled along on the surface, and they hailed her with soft yapping cries, their necks swaying above the surface in the troughs of the waves. Thinking to curry favor, I opened the forward hatch and brought out one of my favorite things — dried *brandade de morue* (mashed salt cod and potatoes) — and scattered it overboard. Their long pointed muzzles curled in disdain. I was disappointed, I passionately wanted them to stay with me, and I'd have done anything to prolong this moment.

One little sea lion, smaller than the rest, was obviously

the group's clown. She romped around the others like a
puppy. I decided she should have a small flying fish that had
tumbled into the boat during the night and lay at my feet.
She gulped it down in a flash, arousing the noisy envy of
her elders. After a while I named her Petula. She had the
sweet look of a little girl, with tiny brown ears and long
lashes veiling her tender, impossibly appealing eyes. The
memory of Petula stayed with me till the end of the voyage, cheering me up on bad days, enlivening my daily log,
establishing an emotional link between the ocean and the
schools back home that had sponsored me.

But Petula wouldn't stay to sweeten my days. Soon
enough, the burning sun brought me to heel. It was mid-
summer in the Southern Hemisphere and the heat was unbearable. The sea lions sought the cooler, deeper waters
below for longer and longer periods. Finally they vanished
altogether. I dreamed of being like them, able to slip
smoothly downward into that darkness, which must surely
be as revitalizing as a draft of cool air. But there was no
question of it, given the risk of sharks, of cramp, of being
unable to climb back on board. It was barely 10 A.M. and
the air was already unbreathable, as thick and cloying as
honey. My hat, protective clothing, and multiple layers of
sunscreen were of no use. The sun had become my worst
enemy, grilling any part of my body that wasn't protected.
Worse, the ocean was now a mirror to reflect it, magnifying
the strength of the rays that assailed me from every side. What
little wind there was to pucker the sea's surface was heavy

and stifling, searing hot like the air in an oven. I tested the water temperature: 81 degrees Fahrenheit! And some days after that it hit 90! Now I understood why the sea lions had fled — the sea had become a boiling cauldron.

I began to worry about running out of fresh water. I remembered my very unpleasant and frightening experience in the Atlantic, when I had to drink salt water mixed with my own urine to avoid dying of thirst. Now each time I started the desalinator I held my breath, straining to hear abnormal noises in its mechanism. I would have to economize on precious water, the elixir without which I would never reach safety.

The paralyzing heat also forced me to organize my energy differently. I rowed for part of the night, early in the morning, and in the late afternoons as soon as the blinding sun sank below the waiting ocean. During the hottest hours of the day, between 11 A.M. and 1 P.M. when it was dangerous to stay outside and risk sunstroke, I reluctantly retreated into my little airless cabin. Buffeted from side to side, suffocating and sweating profusely, I had the hideous sensation of being locked inside a humid greenhouse sticky with salt. The canopy, a few inches above my head, was too hot to touch. Migraines, the bane of my life, surged up; my head felt as if it were clamped in a powerful vise. Each time *Océor* was tossed by the swell I was thrown against the bulkhead, and the drumming in my temples got worse. In tears of grief and despair, I wanted it all to stop, if only for a moment. The roar in my head reached a crescendo. I struggled to calm myself, breathing deeply, drawing the scalding air into my lungs.

Relax. Above all, relax.

The hours that I had to spend in that semi-sealed box were teaching me to extract myself from my surroundings, my body, utterly forget and thus escape. It was a hard lesson. I forced myself to half open my eyes and gaze at the tiny photograph of a waterfall that my mother had sealed in plastic and given to me before I left home. A torrent of fresh cold water splashed down on great glistening rocks. Taped beside my distressingly useless ventilator, the picture embodied my deep yearning for a draft of cool air. I imagined myself far away, sitting amid luxuriant vegetation, in the voluptuous calm of an earthly paradise. And, for a moment, I forgot the oppressive heat. My pulse rate slowed, and I breathed more freely as my mind struggled to escape reality.

The relief was short-lived. A wave lashed against the open hatch and water flooded into the cabin. I sponged it away and immediately received a hammer blow to my right temple: the migraine was still very much present. The day threatened to be a long one. God, I longed for it to end. This was only my sixth day at sea, and already my every fiber yearned for the seventh to dawn. It was hard to relate to time. From one day to the next, I forfeited my customary bearings: the minutes, days, and months had all come to resemble one another in the vast distance I had to cover. I lived with the rhythm of the sun, anticipating its risings and settings.

Monotony set in. I divided the days into hours of rowing punctuated by stretching exercises, massages — such as I could — and other physical attentions. I stopped regularly on the hour to take care of myself, washing, eating, self-exams for incipient boils on my skin, and water filtering. I plotted my position on the map, emptied or filled the ballast tanks that kept the boat trimmed, wrote in my log, and rested. The only moments of relaxation I allowed myself were in the evenings, at dusk. Then, after eating my ration, I would call my home base on the satellite phone to dictate news for the Internet site.

Chantal usually answered. She would have returned from the pharmacy several hours earlier and the family would all wait for my call before going to bed. Our voices echoed, strangely metallic, across the satellite connection, and I remembered how the selfsame tinny sound had accompanied me across the Atlantic. Everything went topsy-turvy inside me at the memory — I glanced at my Pacific map just to reassure myself. *Océor* and I really were in the other hemisphere and fifteen months had gone by since landfall in Spain in October 2003. All was well! Yet those voices . . . I had longed so much to be back with their owners, yet I had opted to leave them again.

Chantal seemed so very far away, on a different planet in a universe I'd left long ago. She told me they'd just finished dinner, making my mouth water with her talk of vegetables — it seemed as if I hadn't tasted a green thing in years. And then she spoke of the weather. Meaux and the

Ile de France were blanketed in snow, while here I was sweltering in my cabin, in unimaginable heat that regularly topped 110 degrees Fahrenheit. Squatting in my cramped quarters, I had barely enough room to poke my head through the hatch and put up the antenna. The merest shift of my hand would cut the phone connection, and I'd have to call all over again — it usually happened two or three times a night. Far away in France, I visualized the phone in the kitchen, close to the radiator and the big oak table. My mother would set herself on the bench with a notepad, and after answering a few questions — her answers would feed my imagination for days after — I would dictate the day's log.

Our talks were too brief to fill the well of loneliness inside me but too long to let me lose myself in the here and now. I have talked at great length about this aspect of solo rowing with Gérard d'Aboville, the great French solo navigator who has helped me immensely with my mental preparation. On his own voyages, he opted for complete isolation, which was his way of protecting himself. If you do that, you enter a bubble of solitude that you gradually adapt to — you don't have to keep coming out of it to field unexpected calls. Actually, contrary to what one might think, communicating with land really isn't a psychological plus. A twenty-minute talk with someone you love will only sharpen the longing for your ordeal to be over. I now understand why teachers ask parents not to call their children when they go away to summer camp. To keep reawakening the heartache of missing somebody is torture, pure and simple.

I switched off the phone, my eyes brimming, then lay back heavily on my damp mattress. I was tightly wedged in, using my elbows to stop my body from banging against the sides, and took a moment to commit to memory everything that had been said. I visualized how they were dressed. What color were Chantal's notepad and pen? What fruit was in the basket on the table? I could see the tiles in the kitchen, picture the quiet alley outside, where a man was walking hand in hand with a little girl. She had a red balloon on a string. That balloon was reminiscent of the clown's nose that hung beside the GPS in my boat — a touch of innocence in my workmanlike, cramped little world. I sat up to catch hold of it and hid it like a talisman in my pants pocket. Thus mysteriously protected, I crawled out of my bed to the cockpit.

The sea was capricious tonight, the waves choppy and chaotic, as if the ocean had a migraine headache just like mine. But my body had to go to work. To forget my heavy head I shut my eyes, extended my arms, drew the oars as far forward as I could and braced my feet on the footboard. My muscles tensed as the blades bit into the water, slowly swinging past me as the boat gained way. *Océor* slid gently onward, bow breasting the waves. My stroke completed, I came forward again and repeated the same movement, over and over, tirelessly. In my need to obey this constant rhythm, I soon forgot my body, which thereafter functioned like a robot. Before long, I had ceased counting my strokes and was observing the stars one by one in the night sky overhead.

The current was carrying me inexorably to the north. My struggle against it was proving largely futile, and the swell was shifting me heavily off my planned course. The thought of all those miles rowed in the wrong direction was crushing — I knew I would have to make up every last one of them with sweat.

Several more hours of rowing passed. It was past midnight, and I noticed that the air was cooler — so much cooler, in fact, that I put on a coat. The night had turned pitch black and I was shivering, though my hands were on fire. I massaged cream into my arms and legs to relax them a little. Then I stood up to stretch and look around and draw breath — and nearly jumped out of my skin.

A ship's lights to port were trained on me. My radar alert hadn't made a sound. This had happened to me on the Atlantic trip. Container ships, assuming there's nobody in their path for miles, don't always keep their radar on. But here, at no great distance from the Peruvian coast, it was a different matter. I quickly noted my course, took a bearing, then didn't look at it for a few minutes with the intent of working out the stranger's trajectory.

When I looked again, no change. There was only one explanation for this — she was coming straight at me. My throat went dry. Why did this have to happen now, in the middle of the night?

I stared hard at the vessel and tried to convince myself that she wasn't moving. But no, she was slowly and stealthily gaining on me. I grabbed my oars, pulled away for a while, looked again, and saw that my visitor hadn't budged. This was incomprehensible. I immediately doused the flashing light on my stub of a masthead as *Océor* and I cowered as best we could amid the sheltering waves. Meanwhile I watched to see what the ghost ship would do next, as I pulled away as swiftly as I could.

Astonishingly, my pursuer's position didn't alter. After two exhausting hours of rowing labor, the situation was precisely the same. I decided to go below and rest a while. I lay in my coffin-like space, my nerves as taut as bowstrings.

The words of the Peruvian navy commandant a few days before my departure were ringing in my head.

"There are pirates cruising off the South American coast."

I was speechless. This was crushing news.

"Do you have a gun aboard?" he went on, gazing absently out of his office window, which overlooked the port of Callao.

At the time, I was feeling rather small, sunk in an armchair deepened by years of service. To cover my distress, I sat up straight like a jack-in-the-box, a dark flush rising in my cheeks. No, of course I didn't have a gun . . . why on earth would I want such a thing on a voyage like this?

Nevertheless, I began to feel misgivings. The commandant sat comfortably in his chair. Was he trying to scare me? Finally he met my stare, and his eyes were kind. He wasn't a tall man; his uniform made him look much more severe than he really was. He was only trying to gauge the strength of my motivation. I explained impassively that I didn't expect to be attacked on the high seas, that the likelihood of another vessel even sighting me was very small, and that I didn't think a weapon, however carefully wrapped against salt and humidity, would be of much use if pirates boarded my little craft at night while I was asleep.

All the same, I knew what had happened to the sailor Peter Black, who was viciously murdered by bandits in 1991 in the course of an expedition up the Amazon aboard his yacht *Seamaster.* Neither his brave crew nor their weapons had been able to avert that tragedy.

The commandant said nothing. Judging by his noncommittal air, he didn't think I had much chance of succeeding, which gave me the creeps. To defuse the situation, I asked him if he knew where I could find detailed charts of the coast close to Lima. At this he brightened — he was happy to be of help. He strode to a big cupboard at the far end of the room, mopping his brow with a white handkerchief. Watching him, I had thought his sweating rather odd, as the office was cool.

*　　*　　*

Océor, heeling in the trough of a big wave, brought me sharply back to reality. The shadow of the unidentified ship still loomed, tied to us by an invisible thread. I wanted her to go away and let me sleep. Also, the unusual blackness of the night was more alarming than I cared to admit. Still, I fought to keep my head clear and above all calm, forbidding myself from ever contemplating any catastrophe. I got up from my coffin and began to row again. It was 3:25 A.M. — stiffness and pirates notwithstanding, I had work to do. Slowly, painfully, I drew away from my unwelcome visitor. I watched as her lights dimmed in the distance, then flicked out one by one to the rhythm of my oar strokes.

And the night closed in once more.

4

Life At Sea

*A*S I LAY IN THE STERN, the moon gleamed through the clear plastic bubble just above my head. The moon was round and full, like the belly of a pregnant woman, rising in a sky of inky black; soft and mysterious, too, with a faint bewitching smile. My eyes closed again, and I fell asleep. For a moment, I left my little *Océor* to drift away to land, which I was already impatient to see again.

Whenever my body and mind permitted, I escaped like this, flying away to meet the people whose presence I missed. I dreamed of catching a look or sharing a smile, of the simple but oh-so-precious happiness of clasping a certain person in my arms. I thought of our shared confidences, words of love and kisses. I also liked to remember the tantrums and furious tirades, which never went further than the end of the dining room table, the emotions we repressed, the misunderstandings, the mad irresistible longings, and the touching weaknesses we shared. All these I missed very much.

On my little boat, when the wind was rising and the sea was angry, when I would rather be anywhere than where I was, I learned to transform myself into a kind of robot. My robot armor, which the ocean had been tempting me day after day to leave aside, could suddenly take over, protecting me, letting me face my difficulties in the most methodical and well-equipped way I could. My ambivalence about my goals when things took a turn for the worse, along with my perfectly average human frailty, remained a continual source of fascination to me. The absence of a partner became a painful emptiness inside me. This voyage was showing me exactly how dependent upon one another we are for nourishment and strength.

Some nights brought nightmares. I heard sinister whispers around the boat. I dreamed I was under attack by mysterious brigands, six men in black trousers cut off at the knee, with faded shirts, broad leather belts, and cutlasses. I waited in the cabin, my heart in my mouth. Their faces beneath their broad-brimmed hats were smeared with soot for camouflage. They looked lost and haggard. The tallest of them came crashing aboard and opened my boxes one by one, looking for something specific. In a flash, I saw what they were after — my desalinator! Terrified, unable to find my voice, I watched as the man took a wrench from his bag and set about unbolting the mechanism. I hurled myself sideways to rock the boat and toss him overboard. *Océor* reared and plunged like a mad horse.

I awoke to find her bobbing on the waves, as usual. There were no pirates above my head, only my dream-catcher, swaying like a metronome. The American Indian dreamcatcher is a kind of spider's web mobile made of leather, feathers, and beads. It's supposed to snare bad dreams, to be burned by the first light of dawn, and preserve good dreams so they can return to envelop you night after night. My dreamcatcher is a present from my father, given to me years ago, and it has brought me plenty of good luck.

Dawn came up stealthily, the first bluish rays of sun-shine spreading across the still-dark sky. I rolled off my pallet and crawled into the open.

At last, a new day!

My first thought was for the wayward Pacific, whose guest I had been for several long weeks. Its velvety blue drew me like a magnet — a part of me always wanted to dive in. The thousands of tiny ripples that puckered the sea's surface gave it a deceptively reassuring, wrinkled and wise look. I felt a wave of gratitude for the tolerance it was showing me.

Each morning, I found myself bidding a friendly good-day to the elements. They were my real companions on this voyage, and somehow imagining them as people filled a corner of my solitude and gave me something to hold on to. Both the sun and the clouds, not to mention the majestic albatrosses and small two-toned fish that kept me company, all heard about what I happened to be thinking. I looked for answers to my daily questions in the faintest breeze or rain shower, in the slightest quickening of the ocean's pulse. The more I observed these things, the more I was able to anticipate their motions and changes and the more I wanted to confide in them and invite them to know me better. I explained what I had come to find here, telling them about the fire in me that was only quenched when I was near them. My voice sounded strange in these vast surroundings. My words went looking for ears to hear them and, with nothing to stop them, wafted softly away on the wind. In my isolation, I felt the certainty of contact with this raw, simple world. The sun might roast my shoulders, but it knew how to calm my fears and warm my heart. Everything around me seemed eager to protect me and give wise advice.

In the cockpit, I found a couple of seven-inch flying fish that had come aboard overnight, attracted by my flashing light. Their backs were electric blue and their bellies silver, with translucent wings like feathery veils.

Flying fish spend most of their lives in the deep waters of tropical and subtropical seas. They feed on tiny plankton and larvae, and they themselves are the prey of swift predators like red tuna and swordfish. When attacked, they explode from the water like silvery flashes of light, propelled by their powerful pectoral fins, whereupon they skim across the surface at a rate of fifty wing beats a minute. I have always been fascinated by these creatures. Why has it been given to them, alone among fish, to grow wings? How did they find a way to escape their enemies by bursting into a new world of blinding sunlight, when other species stay behind to be devoured? Everyday I found this seething ferment of life a marvel.

Today I was joined fleetingly by a pair of albatrosses. Feeding only by day — on mollusks, fish, crustaceans, and other dead creatures floating on the surface — they were delighted by my daily offerings of stale flying fish. Ever since man first ventured out of sight of land, the mighty albatross has haunted his imagination. Its pointed wings — ten feet from tip to tip — make possible its exquisite skill in flight. The albatross has short legs, webbed feet, and a pink hooked beak made up of layered horny plaques. Its plumage is mostly white, with a few black markings, notably on the undersides of its pinions.

The albatross has evolved a gliding strategy that is highly effective and beautiful to watch. It is able to use the air currents and winds with wondrous economy, soaring skyward or diving to the surface of the sea with subtle, almost imperceptible adjustment. It rarely beats its wings, thereby saving energy, though from time to time it may fold them inward to increase its speed or to ride strong winds with greater precision. I spent hours on end watching albatrosses swoop and soar against the blue ocean backdrop, effortlessly following the crests and troughs and guessing the ocean's restive movements in advance. In seas calm or heavy, I enjoyed watching their graceful prowess as they skimmed the waves just inches above the surface.

Once installed on my sliding seat — which by its very design refuses to be still — I returned to my morning routine. First I reached into one of the cockpit boxes for my toilet articles, which I kept in a small white tube with a red top, perfectly watertight. I had brought the absolute minimum: a tube of toothpaste, a hairbrush, an elastic band, baby wipes, a tube of cream, a pocket mirror, anti-salt shampoo, Q-tips, and lip balm — enough to preen myself a little before I bent to the oars. I'd forgotten only one thing, but it was vital, and every morning I was gloomily reminded of it. How could it be, when this voyage had been so carefully thought out, when my every move was being tracked long distance on a chart by Argos, when one of the boat's lockers was filled with a complete set of tools, when every item aboard had been inventoried and checked off twice and thrice . . . how was it that I had no toothbrush?

I still couldn't believe that I had absentmindedly handed it over to Thomas as I was leaving. I realized it was missing the morning after my departure, when a return to port was out of the question.

By another oversight, I happened to have an eyebrow brush among my belongings, which did duty for my teeth during the entire voyage. I considered myself lucky.

Slowly, delicately, the sun drew itself forth from the arms of the horizon. Its rays caressed the ocean with a tender coppery sheen before the first colors of mauve and grapefruit pink began to spread. For a moment, the shafts of light, now ripening to gold, were trapped behind a bank of clouds, while the sky took on a silken texture that banished all memory of the night's alarms. I took a deep breath, untangled my sticky, salty hair, and without more ado unshipped my oars from the cross-rack where I always stowed them when I wasn't rowing. I had a long way to go today. I arched my body for the first stroke of the day.

My sun-parched arms and legs began their rhythmic motion. Showers in fresh water belonged to my past life, and I applied moisturizing cream to my skin only once a day to conserve it. With every stroke, I created small vortexes with my oar blades, which I found hypnotic. They swirl counterclockwise, it seems, in the Southern Hemisphere, clockwise in the Northern.

My body ticked on like a clock that could not stop. To convince myself that time really was passing and I wasn't dreaming, I counted the strokes in my head, one to ten, then started again. Now and then I turned my head in the vague hope, I suppose, of sighting land, but the horizon stayed smooth and unruffled, a wise old man, who seemed to whisper in my ear that there was no hurry. The ocean glistened like a cloth of silver as *Océor* forged onward, her wake closing up behind her. The present was already past, and we were making steady progress.

A milky cloud veiled the sun and the light was softening. I had been rowing for two hours when with a loud electric shriek my radar alarm went off. I stood up and scanned the horizon. The atmosphere turned heavy as *Océor* lost way.

And then I saw a ship, just ahead.

I hadn't heard her on account of the headwind, which drowned the hum of her powerful engines. She was a regular sea bulldozer, a gigantic battleship-gray steel monster — and she was right in my path. She had come out of nowhere in the space of a split second, grinding along at full speed and leaving a trail as broad as a freeway across the swell. Her bow threw out geysers on either side as it bit into the sea.

I slowed *Océor* to a crawl. Being confronted by this 650-foot-long ship was like being transported to another planet populated by giants. *Océor* by comparison was an insignificant speck on the sea surface. And this leviathan was barely thirty yards away! I could only sit there with my mouth open and pray she wouldn't come too close. Given the trouble people had had in locating me in the past even when they knew my exact position, it was certain that this rumbling intruder was completely unaware of my presence a good thirty feet below her. My heart in my mouth, I watched as she mercifully overtook me to steam off into the distance. She was headed west, like me.

No doubt she'd make landfall within a week.

Small puffs of white and pale gray clouds in the sky made me think of Indian smoke signals. I saw them as messages of love from all the people on land who were thinking of me.

★　　★　　★

The more I observed the firmament and the ocean around me, the more adept I became at detecting the smallest changes in their moods. The waves had swollen steadily since the early morning; the boat was staggering drunkenly from side to side, and water had begun to well over her side and slap around my feet. I clung to the oars, continuing to row in my habitual rhythm. I shut my eyes and let my arms and legs do the work, concentrating hard on my action to avoid getting cramps. With each pull I gritted my teeth, listening for the ripple of the sea along *Océor*'s sides. I was in pain from tendinitis, and every morning when I started the day's pulling I did so with the faint hope it had left me overnight. But after a few minutes, the discomfort invariably reemerged in my right thigh with a sharp twinge each time I braced my leg, as if something was crushing the tendon. This had been going on for weeks. It was pressure on the lateral muscle, described to me by doctors as "the tensor muscle of the *fascia lata*." I massaged the place with an anti-inflammatory every time I took a brief rest from rowing, to little avail.

The advice over the satellite phone was to drink a great deal more water. According to my doctor, Jean-Yves Chauves, I needed to take in about seven quarts a day — whereas, in my anxiety about the desalinator's durability, I had been making do with three. The water produced by the desalinator tasted flat and insipid, with no mineral content and no particular taste. It also smelled of the plastic container in which it was stored. I had to force myself to drink it, as one would some kind of evil-tasting medicine.

Moments like these, when the monotony and the sheer constraint of the boat were hard to bear, had become much worse for me, because I could no longer listen to music. I had brought an iPod with me, a gift from my beloved hometown of Meaux, that contained all manner of musical recordings and messages of friendship. For a while it had been a lifesaver. Music lifted me out of myself; listening to words sung and melodies, I put my problems aside. Wearing earphones was like taking a warm, scented bath — reassuring, comforting, and familiar. Each track carried a different memory to dwell on — the children's songs I used to listen to under the bedcovers before I fell asleep, the symphonies and concertos my grandfather took me to hear when my brothers and I went to visit him over the summer holidays, and the hours I spent beside the fire with Tracy Chapman, Norah Jones, and Joss Stone. Music has always been my best tool for insulating myself from the outside world and seeing things clearly.

On my family's boat in the Caribbean, my father often played an alto flute, which he kept carefully wrapped in a sheath of green-and-blue checked fabric made for the purpose by my mother. This was stowed in a special carrying case and was viewed by the rest of us as a treasure to be handled with the utmost respect. I remember how I used to fetch it for him and watch his careful gestures as he brought it out, pausing always to admire the warm tint of the varnished wood. The first tune he played — always at my request — would be "Ce n'est qu'un au revoir" — It's only a good-bye. I never tired of hearing it: every note of the melody was a caress, proof that sweetness could be conveyed through channels far deeper than words. Years later, my eyes would often fill with tears when I heard a piece by Johann Pachelbel or Johann Sebastian Bach. And I still love to shut myself away in my room, dancing alone to rock and roll or country music.

At sea, depending on the music playing on my iPod, I found myself rowing with varying levels of enthusiasm. Richard Jabeneau, who put together my collection, had mischievously included a popular song by Alain Souchon entitled "Rame" (Row). When I listened carefully to the words, it helped me believe that it was truly possible to leave everything behind for this latest adventure.

But alas, my music had come to an untimely end. After only a week on *Océor*, the sea spray proved fatal to the iPod. I opened it and cleaned and dried it thoroughly, but couldn't get it to work again.

As children, my brothers and I had a tape machine. We adored it, but it's hard to imagine what we did to it, how many times it fell out of our bunks when we were listening to tapes of Jules Verne before we went to sleep. Played on that venerable contraption, *Twenty Thousand Leagues Under the Sea* saw us through many a night. It's still working today.

★   ★   ★

I missed my iPod desperately, especially when I had to spend hour upon hour under hatches because of the weather and the risk of capsizing. To help forget it, I started to sing to myself, softly to begin, so as not to rouse the ocean, then more loudly when fear began to take over. While I was rowing, I had Souchon's lyrics on the brain:

> *Rame, rame. Rameurs, ramez.*
> *On n'avance à rien dans ce canoe.*
> *Là-haut,*
> *On t'mène en bateau:*
> *Tu n'pourras jamais tout quitter, t'en aller . . .*
> *Tais-toi et rame . . .*

> Row, row, the boatmen, row
> We're getting nowhere in this pirogue
> Come away, man
> And join the hands
> You'll never know how to chuck it and go
> So shut up and row

The day had been so hot that the sea had produced effervescent clouds of condensation, which were building on the horizon. My watch, as always hanging on the rail of the cockpit, showed 4:45 P.M. I stopped for a moment and curled up under the hatch to enjoy a little shade. The days went by, and little by little I learned to forget my difficulties, to delight in every moment of happiness, however fleeting, whether in simple things or in unforgettable encounters.

I sensed a new presence around me. I heard mouselike squeaks, faint at first, then louder. When I realized what they were, I was overcome with pleasure. Just in time to close this particularly arduous day, they came as a precious reward, undulating gracefully through the waves. I stood up, spellbound. The name dolphin derives from the Greek *delphis,* meaning "spirit of the sea," and it is indeed a fitting one.

A dozen or so of the beautiful creatures were seething around me, nuzzling *Océor* and slapping the water's surface with their tails, splashing water all over me. It was as if I were enveloped in a bubble of magic. They were so close to my little craft I could almost touch them. Their blue-gray streamlined bodies gleamed in the late afternoon light.

Dolphins have smooth, supple skin that adapts to the slightest turbulence in the water around them. With their aqua-dynamic bodies they can swim as fast as 28 miles per hour. They grow to about six feet in length and have elongated noses and beaks with small pointed teeth which they use to catch — but not chew — their prey. Unlike fish, they have horizontal tail fins to propel them with an up-and-down motion. Brazilians and Mauritanians use dolphins in their fishing — the dolphins detect fish shoals and drive them into the nets, whereupon they help themselves in the general confusion along with the men. According to some reports, dolphins are even trained in certain regions to bring boats back to shore when a storm threatens. In my case, though, they seemed more interested in playing with my oars and showing off their astonishing agility.

I clapped my hands and clicked my tongue. They responded with cartwheels.

With each leap, they sprayed *Océor* with water from end to end. It was a beautiful, joyful sight: marine mammals gamboling like children, without a care in the world. One minute they would flash away to port, the next reemerge to starboard, breathless with excitement, poking their heads above the surface for applause. Their smiles were contagious, their simplicity deeply moving. Several times I dipped my hand in the water to caress them, my thoughts flying to the schoolchildren back in France who were conscientiously following my progress and who would have loved to be with me at that moment.

Veering back and forth under the boat, the dolphins kept me company till sundown, after which they vanished one by one, leaving me lost in thought. The sea took on a mauve sheen, like moiré taffeta. The ring of clouds around the sun was delicately laced in pale pink. I glimpsed a flower outlined on the horizon. Night fell gently and peacefully, as if it were glad to return to the ocean's coolness.

5

A Good Catch

AS THE DAYS FOLLOWED ONE ANOTHER, the ocean began to reveal its secrets more readily. I took all the time I needed to observe, feel, and reflect. I advanced, as it were, on tiptoe, noiselessly, trying with every stroke of my oars to tame the universe surrounding me a little further. I began to notice thousands of details that formerly had been hidden. Life slumbered beneath me. It was like my wanderings in the woods at home when I pitied the jogger with his iPod and no inkling of what a person sitting on a rock will wait for hours to experience: hearing the merest crack of a twig, hearing birds breathing or leaves rustling in the breeze. On the Pacific, it was just the same.

I had now seen forty-seven sunrises since leaving the capital of Peru, and I felt like I'd been alone forever. I was less than nothing in this immensity of ocean, which opened itself to me a little more each time I paused to reflect on it. And I was adapting, growing accustomed to a new life untroubled by clocks, superfluities, and deceptions. Tiny ant that I was, new energy and strength made me want to get up each morning and set to work despite my sore buttocks and blistered hands. The sea stimulated me, and in doing so brought back memories of my childhood — happy memories that made me forget my aching body and pull on and on across the waves.

My boat's gentle motion so often reminded me of the years of blissful cruising on our family schooner. When things took a turn for the worse aboard *Océor*, I had only to shut my eyes to see myself as a little girl, crouched in a children's pool by the guard rail, playing with a red plastic ship's wheel lashed to a becket. I learned how to walk on the deck between our two tall wooden masts. Using the deckhouse for support, I made my way to the stays, where I clung on tight, bracing myself for tottering as far as the dinghy housed under the foresail. The distance looked immense, but I was ready to face it alone and unaided.

In its roughness, *Océor*'s cockpit floor reminded me of our schooner's deck covering. My brothers and I used to hop among the squares of nonslip material, and when that surface was too hot for our bare feet, we took refuge under the mainsail boom where there was shade and played with the odds and ends of rigging stowed there. Later, when I was bigger, my favorite place was astride the bowsprit, swinging my legs free and letting the sea splash them for hours as I watched for dolphins.

The best times of all were when we left some port or bay, bound for a new anchorage in a sheltered creek. Then everybody aboard was excited. My mother consolidated everything that might shift or fall during the cruise, while we tidied up our cabin as quickly as possible, stuffing loose possessions into the big locker under our bunks. This done, we went up on deck to watch our father raising the anchor hand over hand like a Trojan, then hoisting the sails and bringing the sheets inboard. He did all this without a word. As soon as the boat was under way, we were allowed to take turns at the helm with our backs to his knobby knees, heroes for a few delicious moments.

During the night I would lie in my bunk and listen to the sea licking softly at the schooner's hull. For me, that sound has always been the most beautiful and effective of lullabies. The music of it was no different aboard my little ocean-going rowboat, and it provided deep nourishment.

At sunrise, the receding horizon was hung with small, sooty clouds. I imagined them as a battalion of soldiers come to protect me from the pirates of my nightmares. Now and then the ocean nipped at their ankles, reminding them to stay alert. Static, imperturbable as guardsmen in the sentry boxes of Buckingham Palace, they stood ready to warn me of approaching danger.

I had a job to do. I needed to transform my long beige trousers, which by now were board-stiff with salt and grime, into a pair of shorts. That way they wouldn't be so irritating to my legs. Working on the pants, I found a couple of *soles,* the Peruvian currency, in a pocket. The little coins bore the emblem of Peru, and they had turned green, like old copper left in an attic. They were of no use whatsoever, except as a subtle reminder of my final days in Lima. I decided to sacrifice them to the sea goddess as a propitiatory offering. With a secret prayer that she would spare me any useless suffering in the weeks to come, I tossed the coins over my shoulder into the ocean.

I settled into my rowing position, and began to think about the book I'd looked at during the night. I had shipped a strict minimum of books and I read each with calculated slowness, drawing them out for as long as possible. *North: Adventures in the Frozen Wild* by Nicolas Vanier, in two volumes, was evocative from its very first paragraph — a world of ice, snow, gallant huskies, and adventures in the frozen north. My fists tightened on the oars as I envisioned the scene in which the river ice shatters beneath the weight of the hero and he sinks into the icy current. He sees his fingers start to freeze before his eyes. . . .

I kept telling myself, *Don't look at that book again till tomorrow. You have to make it last.* This novel, along with Bernard Werber's *Empire of the Ants* and Jean-Luc Van den Heede's *Backwards Around the World,* charmed my leisure moments, allowed me to escape, and spilled over into my dreams. Each volume was carefully stored in a locker and wrapped in a T-shirt against the damp. When I took them out, I handled them like priceless relics of the land.

My principal book treasure, however, was Thor Heyerdahl's *Kon-Tiki and I,* the talisman for my own odyssey. After all, I was following in the footsteps — if you can so describe a sea voyage — of Heyerdahl and his five shipmates, who set out on their balsa wood raft to prove to the world that the civilizations of Easter Island and eastern Polynesia were directly traceable to the great Andean Empire that preceded the Incan. As a child, I had read this magnificent true adventure story time and time again; indeed, it was partly responsible for my own Pacific project.

For Heyerdahl, it all began when he was living on Tetu Hora in the Marquesas Islands and heard an elder telling the ancestral stories of his tribe. The two men talked of Tiki, child of the sun and chief among the gods. Tiki, the mythical ancestor of the Polynesian people, came with his tribe from across the sea to colonize the hitherto uninhabited archipelago. Legend or not, it was beyond doubt that Tiki had come from the east, from a great but very distant land — South America. Many years after he first heard the legend, and after prodigious research, Thor Heyerdahl tracked down the origins of Kon-Tiki, a name from the ancient language of Peru that means "Sun King." The Kon-Tiki he found was the divine leader of a white-skinned people inhabiting the region of Lake Titicaca. Driven out by enemies, he fled westward across the Pacific with his men, their wives, and their children. As far as Heyerdahl was concerned, there was not a shadow of doubt: the Marquesas god and the Peruvian god were one and the same. Kon-Tiki was the real-life father of a civilization from the Andes who left the mountains to conquer the Pacific.

Since nobody was disposed to believe him, Heyerdahl decided the only way to prove his theory was to make the same crossing himself. It took him ninety-one days to steer his raft and his crew intact to the Tuamotu Islands, south of the Marquesas. I planned to make the same landfall more than fifty-eight years later. And not a day passed aboard *Océor* without a thought of those gallant Norwegian adventurers who sailed into the unknown with the most primitive equipment possible and no hope of assistance if things went wrong.

Heyerdahl's stories of the excellent fish he caught — and the constant sight of them hanging around my boat — finally induced me to throw out a line. I had brought along a medallion of the Virgin, presented to me by a diffident Newfoundland fisherman on the Atlantic two years earlier. When I looked at it now, I couldn't help thinking it must have seen plenty of fish go by in the long years its owner had spent at sea. Maybe it would bring me luck today. . . .

The sea life of the Pacific is vast and abundant. Inches beneath my feet were hundreds of little electric-blue fish, hurrying minnows, so many that it looked as though *Océor* had sprouted fins during the night. And today the water around me was a different color — a much clearer, paler blue. The temperature read 77 degrees Fahrenheit, and I thought of all the people back in France heading for the ski slopes. But here in the Pacific I was riding a strand of cool current and there was no doubt that this was the moment to bring out my fishing tackle.

Nicolas, a friend from Papeete, had assembled a fat spool of nylon line to which I could tie five different types of hooks and lures. I selected the smallest hook, which looked pretty big to me. I baited it with a small pilot fish that had darted aboard during the night and ended up on my pillow, then fed line and hook over the side, letting it slip along the hull and taking care to avoid snarling up the tiller. With a hundred feet of line played out, I tied it fast to one of the cleats normally used for the floating anchor.

Now all I had to do was wait.

Sea bream swam in and out of the shade beneath the boat. I never tired of admiring them. You couldn't confuse this species with any other fish, because of their multicolored skin and high foreheads, which made their noses look oddly squashed. Their hues varied from blue to green with occasional golden flashes. They swam peacefully beneath my hull, apparently unaware of me. I lay flat across the cockpit to get a better view of them, and at that moment, with my nose practically in the water, I saw a fin break the surface barely six feet away. I sprang back and stiffened. My first thought was *shark,* but the dorsal fin was much too tall for that — it projected at least a foot and a half out of the water. It was sharply pointed at the apex, lacy at the back, and similar to the fin of a sailfish. I dared not think how big its owner was.

Strangely enough, despite my longing to eat something fresh, this unexpected visitor made me afraid to leave the fishing line in the water any longer. I hastily hauled it in. Naturally, the bait had vanished. There would be no raw bream for lunch today.

I tried fishing several times after that, determined to win a ridiculous running bet with my father that had originated during my Atlantic crossing. "Of course I can fish!" I retorted hotly when he voiced serious doubts about me pulling a mahi-mahi out of the ocean (mahi-mahi is the Polynesian word for sea bream). The conventional wisdom is that you need to be trolling at a minimum of six knots an hour to attract a fish, and since I never got anywhere near that speed with Océor, I was unlikely to catch anything. All the same, given the sheer numbers of fish under the boat, I thought I had a fighting chance.

I was awakened by the patter of rain on my plastic bubble. As a child, I had spent hours watching fresh rainwater streaming down the hatches in wavy rivulets. Rain has the magical power to stop time.

I predicted that the dawning day would be a good

one, cooler than usual. But soon enough — as though its own personal alarm clock had just gone off — the sun leapt from its bed and with a single brushstroke repainted everything with light. There wasn't even time for a rainbow. Once again the ocean was aglitter, and I got a delightful surprise visit from a group of striped pilot fish — a dozen of them, cigar-shaped, moving below me in the clear water. *Océor* had become a kindly protector for these idiosyncratic little creatures, who traveled along under her wing.

I let out the line, and this time it suddenly went taut. My flying-fish-head bait had done its work — too well, as it turned out. I sprang across and grabbed the line, which was cable-tight. I yelled with pain as it sliced into my hand. The blood flowed. Whatever I was connected to was fighting powerfully. My heart started thumping. *Océor* resisted, as if she were afraid this monster — and now it was clear I had hooked a monster — would drag us both beneath the sea.

There was no way I was going to get this creature on board. And now the line was beginning to saw through the cleat to which it was lashed.

I made another effort to maneuver the boat, but the fish was colossally strong. Fearing the worst, I drew my knife from its sheath and prepared to cut the nylon line. I was about to slice when whatever it was managed to pull itself loose and vanish into the deep. Hanging on to the line to keep my balance, I collapsed in the water that had built up in the cockpit.

A few minutes later when I pulled up the hook, I found it bent straight. What kind of creature had taken my bait, I would never know.

The wind had freshened to a gale, and the sea was no longer the same element that comes softly lapping around the roots of coconut trees on paradise islands. It reared and plunged, all-powerful, gnashing its teeth and boiling over the side to sluice around my feet.

Intimidation tactics, I muttered, trying to reassure myself.

A squall was fast developing. *Océor* bucked and plunged as she fought to escape the bigger waves. Meanwhile, my oars kept jamming under the angry surface. It was turning out to be a terrible day after all. I slid off my seat. A series of long swells came rumbling in from the ends of the earth, and I sat there praying they wouldn't swamp me. I shut my eyes and crossed my fingers . . . and they didn't. All around us wave crests foamed and gathered and dispersed like the clouds in the sky, which were banking up apace in interlaced cottony billows. Somehow they lent a note of tenderness to the heaving vastness around me.

It was ten-thirty in the morning by now, and I was hungry. However, there was no orange juice and no steaming hot chocolate aboard, and as usual I had to put aside my craving for vitamins and fruit. I stood up for a moment or two while I waited for a packet of freeze-dried shepherd's pie to rehydrate.

By the time I finished that sad meal the sky was completely obscured. I wondered what kind of blow was about to fall — there's nothing I hate more than sudden weather changes at sea. A great menacing shadow was rushing in my direction, the clouds about to smother me, and the light fled. The waves swelled as though the sky were sucking them upward; the squall came tearing across the surface, plowing great furrows into which *Océor* lurched and staggered.

I was determined to stay in the open, if only to rinse off the layer of salt that now covered me like a second skin. I clung to the oars to keep from being swept overboard, and before I had time to do anything else, the downpour hit me in a solid sheet. The sea became perfectly white, smoking and bubbling before my eyes. Heavy rain lashed my skull. Like the ocean, I bowed my head before this onslaught, but the rain actually seemed to have come to my assistance; its effect was to flatten the waves. Still, torrents of rain washed over me, the raindrops bouncing off the surface of the sea as if off parched earth. The ocean was playing tough, but the raindrops were patient, redoubling their effort. Before long, the tumult abated, and in its place came a long easy surge. The ocean had drawn in its claws. The sky acknowledged its surrender, and the rain abruptly ceased.

It was over.

I raised my head, rubbed my hair with a towel, peeled off my T-shirt and hung it up to dry. In the blink of an eye, the sky had turned clear blue again as the sun returned to illuminate the vast Pacific. I took a deep breath and leaned over the side to seek a little serenity in contemplation of the world beneath me.

The pilot fish were still there, and beyond them the unfathomable depths. I was bewitched by the harmonious dancing of the waves, now tamed by the storm. The water moved before me like a rippling rattlesnake, or so it seemed to me.

Beware, it seemed to whisper. *Beware.*

I dipped my hands watchfully in the water. It was warm and comforting.

I caught sight of a big bream circling the boat a few yards away. I looked at it hungrily. No doubt about it, as a fisherman I was a complete flop. I wondered why.

But next morning a big flying fish blundered into the cockpit and changed everything. I hadn't had a scrap to eat since the night before, and this time I was determined to succeed. I got out the tackle, baited the hook with the flying fish, paid out the line, and watched my glittering bait sink beneath the surface.

Forty minutes later I got a serious bite. The line tightened and I leapt on it, knife at the ready. But this time the fish was manageable. With the utmost care I brought him alongside, fighting hard. I knew sea bream were strong and didn't give up easily. I'd forgotten whatever else I knew: nothing else mattered at that moment but the fish and me.

He showed, finally, and indeed he was a handsome mahi-mahi, about twenty inches long. At last I'd have some fresh meat, provided he didn't fall off the hook at the last moment.

The swell was no help in the next tricky maneuver. On my haunches, braced in the cockpit, I gently drew my catch clear of the water and over the side. He dropped at my feet, flapping wildly, soaking me in the process.

The water in the scuppers was suddenly dark with blood. It was difficult getting the hook out of my sea bream's mouth, and I had to be careful not to cut myself on its dorsal fins. The acts of killing and gutting were delicate, almost surgical, but I performed them willingly, with the promise of eating something worthy to be called food.

Soon fillets of delicious firm white flesh were drying on my solar panels.

Sashimi for lunch!

My fishing excitement over, I now had to face an unwelcome fact: the weather forecast provided by my team on shore had been defective. I needed to do something about it.

I could already see more threatening clouds in the sky, like a roving mob of Blackshirts looking for trouble. The sulky sea appeared to be covered in a fine layer of dust. It looked restive, its breathing staccato as it scraped against *Océor*'s hull, making her lurch and jump. Meantime, the wind gusted strangely across the angry wave crests. Trying to keep a low profile, I advanced tentatively through this swirl of ill humor, but found no escape. I had to meet the truth squarely.

The sea is like that. It doesn't bother to ask your opinion. At sea, you have to be prepared at any moment to forsake your ordinary human veneer and wrap yourself in the simple animal instinct to hang on — and then hang on some more. You have no way of knowing how high the waves will be or how long the storm will last. Your only certainty, which you can repeat to yourself for comfort, is that it will eventually end. And that's all.

The sea began its assault and *Océor* began her resistance. I hastily drew in my oars, made them fast and scuttled below, securing the hatch behind me. The waves swelled steadily, as I watched them anxiously from within. My little craft was tossed hither and thither, and from where I crouched it felt as if we were being rolled and dragged across rough gravel. Everything creaked and shuddered around me. I clung for dear life to the handles set in the bulkhead. The rudder bar banged from side to side, echoing in my head. I wanted to scream, to somehow to make the banging stop.

Several times the cockpit got completely swamped, and once water poured through the tiny crack of the hatch I'd briefly opened to breathe, soaking everything around me.

Flat on my stomach, I grabbed a bowl and started bailing out the seawater that had flooded into my tiny quarters — but just at that moment a massive wave rolled the boat vertically on her beam ends. My head smashed against the wall and, with an instinctive reflex, I flung my weight to the other side to bring the boat back into kilter and stop her from capsizing. Obediently, *Océor* righted herself.

Around me everything was chaos. My red clown's nose was afloat, my roll of paper towels was dissolving before my eyes, all sorts of equipment had been projected out of the lockers and were sluicing to and fro in a liquid mess that the sea refused to take back. I seized my sodden pillow as it went by. Luckily, the little gas burner had stayed in place.

At moments like these, haunted by faces of the people I loved, I wished with all my heart to be with them.

The night was unending. I battened down the hatches, cutting off air to breathe. The heat in that confined space was stifling; sleep was out of the question. As *Océor* battled on against the elements, I did my best to wedge my body in place with my knees so I wouldn't bounce around. The tendinitis came back with a vengeance — I wept with pain.

Hours later, the moon began to glimmer among the clouds, and I was able to open the bubble to breathe fresh air again. It rose in a veil of voluptuous apricot, as I watched timidly from behind my Perspex bubble, praying it would never go away again.

By morning, only a few white and gray clouds remained. They sat on the horizon, forming the shape of an anvil — the last shreds of a storm that had lasted for many hours. A few lemony shafts of light were already showing in the east.

Soon it would be day.

6

Halfway

MY FACE WAS NUMB WITH COLD as I groped through a thick, milky fog, with visibility down to a few feet. *Océor* was utterly lost, drifting palely among the Grand Banks of Newfoundland. And I was exhausted: rowing was getting me nowhere. The boat was locked in a mighty current, which had been pushing it steadily back on its tracks for several days. Covered with icy droplets, sunk inside my hooded oilskin coat, I soldiered on. Suddenly I felt the boat strike something hard in the water. . . .

I awoke with a start.

No, that can't be land. We're not there yet. . . .

Over and over again, dreams from my earlier crossing came to haunt my nights. Apart from the heat, the Pacific differs from the Atlantic because of its mighty swell, a long, broad-backed undulation from the south that sweeps the whole vast ocean. *Océor* and I were ceaselessly battered and shaken by it. I seldom managed more than forty-five minutes of sleep at a stretch. In fair weather or foul, I was never able to contemplate the beautiful Pacific without this swell, making the water around me seem like mountains on the move. But the Pacific offered a major difference from the Atlantic: birds, fish, and animals were far more present and vividly broke the monotony of my days.

As for my little boat, it was just the same. What had changed was my state of mind. The 2003 experience was invaluable in preparing *Océor,* my equipment, and myself. I could better anticipate the difficulties; I left port far better armed and more seasoned. I had proved — and proved to myself — that I was a tough nut, and now I was able to proceed more smoothly, in a more human, sensitized way. I had set aside my armor, and learned to marvel at my surroundings like a child.

It was ten past two in the afternoon. I was lurking like a rabbit in my hutch, waiting for the sun's heat to abate a little. As usual, the heat was a terrible adversary. In the cabin, where it hit 110 degrees, I could only lie flat on my back with my feet wedged in the plastic bubble above me to keep the blood circulating. I still hoped to cure my tendinitis with anti-inflammatory cream and massage on my right thigh, but it never seemed to get any better.

My precious sunglasses and white baseball cap hung from one of the rope rails around the cabin. I glanced at my active-echo radar; it was blinking green. No ships in the offing. Forced by necessity to lie there and breathe the unbreathable, I fought off my umpteenth migraine attack.

Still an hour to wait before I could go back to the fresh air, and my temples were throbbing.

At last I climbed out and took my position on the sliding seat, my back against the hatch. I gazed at the horizon. The ocean's deep blue was blended with the lighter tone of the sky. *Océor* and I were suspended in space, the burning sun above us our only point of reference.

> Date: February 19, 2005
> Day Number: 38
> Latitude: 7° 46' 26" South
> Longitude: 107° 46' 04" West
> Wind speed and direction: 15 knots, SSE
> Sea: Long swell, troughs 1m50
> Weather: Sunshine, a few low clouds toward evening
> Number of nautical miles covered since leaving port: 1,833 (3,395 km)
> Distance covered today: 60 miles (111 km)
> Noteworthy events: Halfway mark reached! Immense joy!
> Special note: I am changing the gas bottle on my little burner.

I could hardly believe it. Halfway! Sheer delight engulfed me. From the bottom of my heart, I shared that delight with every soul who had believed in me.

The dream may have been my own to start with, but I knew it would never have gotten off the ground without the many protectors who had thrown their weight and their sense of wonder behind me. These friends weren't the kind who just smile and wait and see. On the contrary, they rolled up their sleeves and helped me to move mountains, shift shiploads of incredulity, and pick myself up again when everything seemed to be going awry.

My thousands of oar strokes were theirs as well.

I looked around me: knowing that I was right at the middle made my heart swell. I felt so insignificant compared to this vast expanse of ocean, with twenty thousand leagues beneath my feet and nothing but blue waves and sky as far as my eyes could see. My head swam with the grandeur of it.

I felt the ecstasy of one who is both utterly alone and utterly free. Free of the beaten track, freed by the pledge I had made to do this, free of the imaginary leaden shackles by which we all think we are held.

If, as I believe, happiness lies in being where we have dreamed of being, then I was happy for those hours. The sea airs and vapors seemed to have cleansed my boat and me of the dusty past. I forgot the weeks of backbreaking work it had taken to reach this point, and all the unavoidable moments of discouragement. Gone for the moment were the migraines, the rampaging waves, the constant tendinitis, and the rib that refused to mend. The ocean had carried them all away. Simpler and cleaner, my body and soul had been reunited with their true essence and direction through confrontation with the raw elements.

This was why I had rowed so far and so long! The sea's noble, velvety blue seemed to be sighing through a multitude of foamy ripples. Every day I felt myself more a part of it. Together we were pursuing the same mysterious, unreachable horizon.

I closed my eyes.

The atmosphere around me was devoid of scent or smell. The ocean had washed everything clean, as if it meant to make itself completely neutral. Because the ocean troubles you so little with complications, it helps you to see the simple sources of your happiness in sharper relief.

When I rubbed cream on my skin, for example, I would see myself at home in the bathroom, emerging relaxed and perfumed from the shower, wrapping myself in a fresh bath towel. Every freeze-dried meal of the voyage contained at least one spice that could carry me back to the delicious cooking smells wafting from my mother's kitchen. Spaghetti alla carbonara, even in powdered form, retains the smell — if not the look — of bacon and onions frying in the pan. I heard the whirr of the hood, the water boiling, the faint rustle of pasta decanted from package to pot. And on days when my food was barren of mental associations, tube samples of eclectic smells, prepared by my brother Roch, made up for it. Whenever I chose, I could smell the tobacco of one of Marc's cigars, or mint crystals like the ones my mother used to bring home from the pharmacy, a pinch of the curry powder I use in many of my favorite dishes, the scent of wild blackberries like the ones at the far end of my grandfather's garden, and other harmonious blends of familiar odors.

As for colors, there was little else but blue on the Pacific, and perhaps the white of the few clouds that sometimes brought me shreds of shade. The entire universe seemed to consist of variations from the same pot of paint.

Océor bobbed on the waves. Flying fish were all around us now, small shoals like silver rays flashing across the surface. The days blended into one other, and my solitude grew steadily harder to bear. Nevertheless, I knew I wasn't totally alone in the middle of the Pacific. Hundreds of miles to the north of my position, above the Equator, was the tiny mysterious island of Clipperton. Jean-Louis Etienne was there at that very moment with a group of researchers, carrying out a study of the island's ecosystem. His results, God willing, would make it possible to establish firm guidelines for the protection of Clipperton's biodiversity. There was no way I could turn aside and visit him — we were too far apart. Nevertheless, his relative proximity was reassuring.

I forged on. *Océor* and I were well on the way now, and I had opened the second flap of my chart. Obviously I hadn't reached the last summit in terms of effort. This was no bicycle ride and there would be no long, effortless descent. On the contrary, the next days and weeks would be every bit as hard as the ones that had gone before. My course into the unknown was set for a long time yet. In the Tour de France, I imagine that when the competitors reach the halfway point they feel like they're headed for home. In my case, I was moving geographically farther away. But I had won half a victory, and I had the joy of telling myself

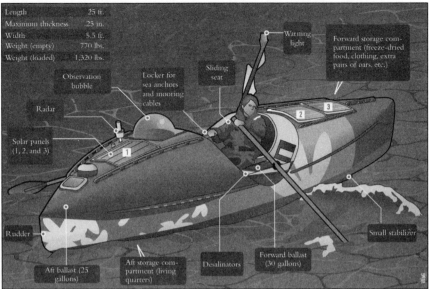

Length	25 ft.
Maximum thickness	.25 in.
Width	5.5 ft.
Weight (empty)	770 lbs.
Weight (loaded)	1,320 lbs.

Warning light

Forward storage compartment (freeze-dried food, clothing, extra pairs of oars, etc.)

Sliding seat

Observation bubble

Locker for sea anchors and mooring cables

Radar

Solar panels (1, 2, and 3)

Rudder

Small stabilizer

Aft ballast (25 gallons)

Aft storage compartment (living quarters)

Desalinators

Forward ballast (30 gallons)

Final inventory on the floating pier of the Callao Yacht Club in Lima, Peru: 600 lbs. of material, including 3 pairs of oars, 1 survival outfit, flares, 2 desalinators, 2 GPS locators, 1 portable VHF radio, marine maps, 2 Argos beacons, 1 satellite telephone, 1 repair kit, 1 toolbox, 300 feet of rope, 260 lbs. of food, 1 first-aid kit, 1 portable stove and reserve gas canisters, 1 fishing line, 55 lbs. of clothes, 3 books, 1 camera, and 1 iPod.

January 12, 2005, 6:10 P.M. local time: departure, a feeling of excitement and concern.

Océor's christening by Patrick Poivre d'Arvor, accompanied by my young adventurers, happier than ever.

Long hours of rowing under a scalding sun,
blue as far as the eye can see.
Ahead: almost 4,500 miles.

A blister on every finger,
until my calluses form.

Ten cubic feet of space: my tiny
living quarters, decorated with
children's drawings.

Once a day I allow myself to study the marine
maps. My actual daily distances are laughable
compared to the course.

One of many sunsets, the charming colors always brought a smile to my lips.

Chance meeting with dolphins, a moment of happiness, innocence, and harmony with Nature.

During the night a flying fish dropped into my cockpit. Breakfast!

After 73 days of freeze-dried food, I dreamed of a hearty salad, fresh fruit, and mouth-watering orange juice . . .

Another day of foul weather. Huge waves come washing into *Océor*. Inside, everything is soaked. I'm suffocating. I hang on tight and wait . . .

A surreal moment: alone for months, suddenly I receive an unexpected visit: the frigate *Prairial* hoves into view.

Ninety men on board send me their greetings. A helicopter circles above *Océor*. The captain asks if I'm all right. I'm flabbergasted!

Rowing toward my dream with the ocean floor 1,000 to 2,000 fathoms below me.

Rowing 8 to 10 hours a day, in search of that
freedom and purity the ocean offers me.

Rounding the tip of Hiva Oa. About 2 A.M. I light my flares, and at sunrise I row to meet the Polynesian outrigger that has come to meet me.

On the beach, an emotional reunion with my mother, Chantal, surrounded by virtually the entire island population.

Two Marquesans fetched me from *Océor* and carried me to the beach.
I felt both elated to have succeeded and excited to be back in the world.
I dedicate this victory to all those who believed in it and me.

Crowned with a lei by Oscar Temaru, the president of Polynesia, who with his entire government receives us warmly.

© C. Durocher

© Roch Fontenoy

A souvenir photo with friends, the entire crew of the *Tapageuse*, the navy boat that sailed out to greet me upon my arrival.

© C. Durocher

Together with my mother and Jacqui Drollet, literally covered with garlands of intoxicating flowers, I'm in seventh heaven. One of the most beautiful moments of my life.

that whatever happened from here on, at least I'd done half the distance. In a way, it was almost symbolic that Polynesia had suddenly become accessible.

I remembered Gérard d'Aboville's advice: "Don't even let yourself think of arriving till you're past halfway. Not a moment sooner, Maud!"

And now I had covered 2,200 miles, with the same distance to go before I made landfall. I dreaded a nightmare scenario whereby I would somehow be blown back behind this point. That had happened three times in the Atlantic, and it had been pure torture. I had raged at the injustice of it, of losing those precious days. Now I had to keep in mind that I was still at the mercy of technical problems, sudden weather changes, major health concerns.

It is never a good idea to linger in the desert, whether it be one of sand or water. I couldn't afford to get in trouble here, thousands of miles from the rest of my species. If I suddenly needed help, it would take the nearest ship at least ten days to reach me.

I'd never had my appendix removed. My doctor's advice was to leave it alone, since the postoperative complications could be just as bad as appendicitis itself. When worry about it entered my head, which was fairly often, I immediately banished it. To entertain the fear of bad luck only serves to attract it. Perhaps I'm superstitious, but in any case, I have to believe my method works.

Touch wood: I've never had any health crisis of the sort on the high seas.

To celebrate my thirty-eighth day at sea, there was no champagne, no can of foie gras — only a small plastic pouch that I drew carefully forth from my electrical supply box. Clutching this treasure, I sat myself comfortably in the shade of the forward hatch. The pouch contained a trove of letters from my friends, family, from people who had wanted to accompany me for part of the voyage. On one of them was an unambiguous notice: *Not to be opened till halfway.* And here I was. I took it out, my hand trembling with impatience, savoring the moment as one might a chocolate bar. Then I opened it, spinning out the pleasure for as long as possible.

It contained a postcard, with a black-and-white photo of a narrow paved alley lit by a ray of afternoon sunshine. In the foreground, the terrace of a small café, with chairs and tables. A man was walking by with a chair on his shoulder. Within seconds, I had totally forgotten the sea: instead I heard the clatter of glasses and the hum of bar talk. On the back of the card were just two words: *Reviens vite!*

Crouched over my oars, a pygmy in a world of giants, I was learning the hard lesson that in our daily lives it is impossible to fully comprehend the multitude of things that happen to us, the endless stimuli that our novelty-hungry brains receive from the outside. From the advertising billboard in the street to the next meeting, by way of ringing telephones and lists of things to do, we are constantly in demand whether we are aware of it or not. On my tiny craft, in a world without bearings or references, there was none of this. I lived on what I had, rummaging each morning for fresh resources in the attics of my past life or inner self and praying those resources wouldn't run out.

My imagination and my five senses had awakened from a long sleep, as if carried by adventure back to the core of life.

Day after day, I followed the variations of the sounds surrounding me. The wind: how it whistled through the porthole left ajar, how it snapped my two small flags, one the obligatory French tricolor, the other the arms of the City of Meaux. And the sea; its muted drumroll of water beneath *Océor*'s fragile skin, a dull sound as if one was momentarily deafened. I also listened for hissing and slapping against the bulkhead, or groaning. More unnerving were the growls of the waves that snapped at my oar blades and the premonitory slither of the ones that unexpectedly burst into the cockpit and drenched me with spray. But next morning at first light, I would swear the sea was whispering softly, as if begging my pardon for the awful night it had put me through.

This was where I lived now — in a world I had to adapt to if I was ever to reach my destination.

Algae had begun to collect on the floor of the cockpit and on the lifeline (the line that attached me to the boat at all times when I was outside the cabin), which always lay there. The closer I got to the Polynesian islands, the warmer the water; the shallow liquid under my seat was like a plant nursery. Every morning, as soon as I was awake I scrubbed it down with an abrasive sponge, but the green stuff kept coming back. The resultant viscous, slippery carpet was dangerous underfoot.

I imagined that *Océor*'s bottom was in no better shape.

The day drew to a close and the sea turned an unaccustomed mauve. Its mood must be about to change. I was right. As night fell the sky rapidly clouded over. There would be no moon tonight.

Suddenly the radar detector let out a series of shrill shrieks. At first, I thought I hadn't heard right. Out here in the very middle of the Pacific, it was highly unusual to see another vessel. But then the alarm screeched a second time.

I scanned the horizon. Visibility was considerably reduced, but it still wasn't dark enough to show a ship's navigation lights. The red light was still blinking and I concluded she was hidden in the waves. Then *Océor* rose high on the swell and I sighted her.

I hastily pulled on my shorts and got out the binoculars. A gray floating monster was steaming straight for me; clearly it had no idea I was there. The tension rose — insofar as I could, I paced my quarterdeck. This ship was staggeringly huge. Meanwhile, my radar alarm got louder. Something was terribly wrong.

Then a second ship, and a third, loomed. Incredulous,

I rubbed my eyes with my knuckles. I must be smack in the middle of a shipping lane, though nothing had indicated that on the pilot charts. Before long, I could see their lights clearly, like the crafts from outer space in H. G. Wells's *War of the Worlds*.

Since they were steaming in the same direction I was, I could only wait and hope they wouldn't pass too close.

Luckily, the southern swell was doing its best to keep us hove to and drifting out of the ships' path. Even so, I rowed northward to make sure the gap was as wide as possible. The three enormous freighters took about two hours to quit my field of vision. Determined and all-powerful, they forged past without even bothering to notice me. And here I had been fantasizing that I might just lay eyes on another human being!

After this, things were clearer in my head. If I was going to see people again, it would be in Polynesia, where there were plenty waiting for me. One intrepid star winking above the clouds seemed to be shining brighter than the rest — perhaps it was watching over me.

But shadows had gathered on the sea, and at this point I dared not give free rein to my imagination. I had to rest before the next alert. If I really was in a shipping lane, there would be plenty more visitors as the night wore on.

I opened the hatch a little wider and settled down, forcing myself to breathe deeply and regularly, hoping to relax and get some sleep.

Every hour I woke up to scan the horizon; some ship

might be approaching without radar. Twice the alarm went off and called me to my action station, oars at the ready. My eyes were stinging with fatigue as I scanned the navigation lights, my only way of calculating the courses and intentions of the vessels around me.

I could imagine life aboard those ships. Most of the sailors would be snoring in their soft bunks. The rest would be taking their watch, on the lookout for other ships, never for a moment imagining that a tiny two-armed creature like me, gesticulating wildly, might be anywhere nearby.

I kept rowing.

But . . . something was wrong. The rudder was stuck to port. Something must have jammed in the mechanism. I hoped the cable hadn't snapped. I shifted it, gently at first, then more vigorously, beginning to sweat with anxiety. No movement.

Come on, Océor, this isn't the moment to let me down. Please don't let me down now!

I took a deep breath. The first thing was not to break something and make the problem worse. Patience, Maud. I started again — a yank to starboard, a yank to port, keeping a weather eye on the supertanker bearing down on me with all its lights blazing. One more time, once to port, once to starboard. . . .

There! I felt the mechanism break free and the rudder blade swing to the other side. I heaved a deep sigh of relief. Then I made the rudder fast in case a wave tried to slam it in the other direction.

★　　★　　★

The sun was up at last, dissolving the memory of that terrifying night. My face in the mirror was drawn with tension and I was stiff in every joint. With every move, my tired muscles made me wince; I was paying a price for the long night hours of rowing. A colossal hand seemed to have squashed my arms and legs. I dragged myself out of the narrow cabin and tried to stand for a while in the cockpit. Lord, would I have loved a hot shower, a massage, even a comfortable chair at that moment!

Overhead, a few sooty clouds remained of the night. All the rest was blue blended with tenderest pink. The sun floated from its ocean couch and, motherlike, caressed my face and aching shoulders.

I noticed that the cockpit was emptying less; the scuppers that drained it looked blocked. I hunted for a tool to give them a good cleanout, but could find nothing better aboard than the aluminum handle for working the ballast pumps. Once the algae was cleared away, I discovered several shellfish growing in the narrow passage.

This was a nasty surprise. If the scuppers were clogged like this, the state of the hull must be something horrid. I leaned overboard as far as I dared to get a closer look at the enemy, but the boat tilted with me and nearly pitched me into the sea.

After several attempts, I managed to get a hand underneath and pulled off a shellfish over an inch long. There was no doubt of it now: *Océor* was covered in unwelcome stowaways. Sooner or later I'd have to go in the water to remove them.

On top of that, I was seriously concerned — although I preferred not to think about it — about the rudder. For once, I would have preferred this problem remain a nightmare, not reality.

By now the wind had shifted, and the forward steering mechanism was no longer sufficient to keep *Océor* on course. Since I was now alone on the ocean again and able to zigzag as much as I liked, I nervously released the tiller.

This time the rudder blade was completely jammed! No doubt about it. I slumped on my sliding seat and racked my brains.

I had very few options. If the rudder answered yesterday, it meant the cable was still intact. So there was something else in the way. Either the problem was in the water, in which case I'd have to take my courage in my hands and jump into the sea, or else it was somewhere in the bulkhead and unreachable — a total disaster.

My best hope was that shellfish were causing the trouble. Yet the idea of struggling to clean them off, with miles of ocean beneath, was not exactly enchanting. I suddenly remembered the sharks I'd seen earlier. I'd hate myself if something went terribly wrong.

Once again I was alone, wrestling with a decision on which my survival hinged, looking in vain for some kind of help from the universe.

7

Further Encounters

*T*HERE SHE BLOWS!
Less than forty yards away, a geyser blasted powerfully from the surface.

Dead ahead, the mighty back of a whale in the waves. I watched, pulse racing, legs jelly, as it undulated toward me in slow, immaculate movements, seemingly unaware of my presence. I'd never seen a whale so close before.

It's blue-black body was at least three times the length of my boat. It probably weighed about a hundred tons. Rather foolishly, I wondered what to do. With a single flap of its tail, it could easily crush my little *Océor* and send her to the bottom. Nevertheless, the calm gentleness exuded by this largest of the world's living creatures somehow reassured me — and encouraged me to make no sudden gestures as it slowly came closer.

Maybe the whale was just as disconcerted as I by this encounter. Who knows? But it was as if together we were entering, the whale and I, an indescribable space between our respective worlds. Existence consisted of the ocean, this gigantic cetacean, and my frail rowboat. All about us was quiet. Even the wind had dropped; the sea itself was in suspense.

Unperturbed, the whale forged through the waves, engulfing as it went huge quantities of water, which it then rejected through the baleens of its great mouth. The baleens filtered the plankton, sardines, and other small sea creatures that were its food. Whales are endangered in certain parts of the world because men still hunt them intensively for their blubber!

I slipped my hand into the warm water, trying to relax, to loosen the muscles of my body as much as I could. Somehow I wanted the ocean to convey my peaceful intentions. I wanted my fingers to speak to the whale, warn it of my presence, and perhaps induce it to stay awhile. I even wanted to join it, to become a whale myself for a few moments and understand what went through its head when it spied *Océor*'s hull bobbing on the surface.

We were barely fifty feet apart. My only concern was that there might be a stupid accident.

Then the whale discreetly raised its head and took a furtive look at me.

This totally charmed me, and I drew a deep breath of air into my lungs. The whale didn't look at all upset, and the movement of my hand in the water hadn't made it change course in the slightest. We were both at roughly the same level in the water and it was still edging gradually toward me.

Then I had the impression there was a slight acceleration. The whale began to look for all the world like a combine harvester moving ponderously down a field of corn. I felt a rush of adrenaline, and my throat went dry. Was I going to survive this? I pulled hard on the oars, but already it was too late. In a moment the thing would be upon me. . . .

Instead, with a colossal writhe of its body, it dived. For a few moments I watched as the great dripping tail rose clear of the surface, described an arc, and got swallowed in the water beneath *Océor's* stern. The very sea seemed to vibrate, and then . . . nothing. The ocean, perfectly indifferent, recovered its former tranquillity.

Thirty feet ahead the whale suddenly and gracefully broke the surface again, loudly blew the water from its lungs, and bore away southward.

This episode left me thrilled, relieved, and awestruck all at once; tears brimmed in my eyes. The ocean had deigned to reveal another of its secrets, and whatever the price the moment was worth it. For a good while now the Pacific appeared to have forgotten all about me. The longer we spent on her surface, *Océor* and I, the more we were absorbed into her noble family.

It was 11 A.M., and to my hungry eyes the sky resembled a macaroon, a thick, veined layer of white cloud cover, from which a stream of blue occasionally poured. It made my mouth water, and the ocean, more greedy even than I was, seemed to be biting lustily into this delicious horizon. The sea had never been so beautiful. It shone and glittered, playing artlessly with the breeze and the flying spindrift. I leaned on my oars in a fit of melancholy, reliving the magic moment with the whale and thinking of the faraway children who were following my progress.

In my ship's log, which was posted daily on the Internet, I shared every day of my voyage and every encounter like this with the children. I knew how much they would have loved to have been with me today, the children from the Hôpital d'Avicenne, the schools in the housing estates of Meaux, Sarreguemines, Paris, Polynesia, and elsewhere. I had always insisted on associating children with my challenges, making concrete suggestions for learning projects to teachers and principals. From the very first weeks of preparation, I would be in classrooms before scores of attentive eyes, trying to transmit in the simplest possible way my enthusiasm, my desire to achieve a goal, my taste for effort and perseverance, and above all my need to make my dreams come true — those dreams that are latent in all of us and which we must never allow to die.

Often, when we are small and express aloud our early yearnings, we get ready-made replies such as: "Darling, that's just not possible! You're not strong enough, not good enough in school. That's not for you. . . ." At which point our pretty little heads droop, and the wings that were beginning to sprout wither away.

Every day at sea, I tried to drive home the idea that the energy we need to accomplish any project, anything we like, big or small, alone or in company, on land or sea, is waiting inside each one of us, waiting to be used. To my mind, the secret of success resides in two great things: work and confidence in your own ability.

Whatever their background, class, or native country, the most fascinating thing about the world's children is their insatiable curiosity, and their way of always asking *how*.

Whereas adults seldom think beyond *why*.

From the length and design of my oars to the workings of my ballast pump system, from the use of my GPS to the size of the sharks I've sighted, I have been asked every possible question by children. Once they were through with the technical details, they would turn to the subject of my mother, whom they tried, I suppose, to identify with their own; and then they would interrogate me closely about my fears and how often I cried. They couldn't get enough of all this, and our talks would continue on and on, perhaps over a cake in the shape of a heart they had all baked together. After my talks, extraordinary drawings, collages, paintings, and other artwork would arrive in my mailbox, things the children had devised especially for *Océor*'s little cabin such as a picture of my boat with four oars, or of a dolphin pulling it; or of me, with a big shining sun sitting on my shoulders.

And then there was *Océor*'s official christening, which allowed lots of children to see her close up. After that, there was the day she was packed into her travel container which they watched on video, and then came the moment for me to leave.

Day after day, each class followed my progress and worked in a playful, interactive way on the different themes associated with it. Each Wednesday a school in Paris prepared a research page on a given subject for the Internet site, which was later used as backup by the others. The teachers in both France and Polynesia did a remarkable job of integrating every detail of my crossing with the usual school program. For example, in French classes they worked on travel literature and sea poetry. In mathematics, they studied latitude and longitude. In physics, they talked about every aspect of water, sea currents, desalination, wind power, and so on, covering every different subject.

In the class presided over by Madame Busson — a person who is remarkable for her charisma, devotion, and gift for constantly getting the best out of children — the pupils at Pierre Colinet primary school were able to make serious progress in the fields of writing, reading, and geography. Every morning, my log was uploaded to the site and read aloud so everyone could understand. The vocabulary was then dissected and careful research work done on flora, fauna, weather, distances, and Easter Island. I think those ten-year-old children now know more than I do about the lives of sea lions in their natural environment, not to mention the techniques used by Polynesians to catch flying fish.

At the Avicenne Hospital in Pantin, on the edge of Paris, I was in contact with the pediatric oncology department run by Dr. Nicole Delphine. Here children and teenagers suffering from rare cancer conditions were fighting against their terrible illness. I admired their strength of will and character, their sheer positive energy. And since I had no other way of helping them to overcome their illness, I tried — by visits to the hospital, and by behaving in the most human way I could — to bring them something of the freedom of the open sea.

Every Tuesday in the early afternoon, I was on live radio. Thanks to *Wind Report,* everyone who wanted to — children, journalists, friends, family — could connect at the same time and ask me questions for about fifteen minutes. Today was that day, and I was so impatient to hear from the kids at the Guynemer School in Paris that I turned on the satellite phone at least fifteen minutes before the appointed hour.

While I was waiting, I relieved the staggering heat of the day by bathing my feet in the sea and — since I couldn't jump in — splashed myself all over. The sun's rays pierced the surface and vanished in a cone of light far below me. I stayed watchful, however, hastily withdrawing my legs at the least sign of anything suspicious.

The telephone rang. I scrambled inside and picked up the handset.

Bonjour. It was the voice of a very small child, a delight to hear.

Grinning from ear to ear, I savored every peal of laughter, the song composed for the occasion, and an "Ode to Petula," the sea lion that had followed me at the start of the voyage.

At the end of our conversation, the kids proudly announced that on Friday my mother would be back again at the computer center at Meaux to answer their questions. Judging by what they said, they expected to have plenty of fun with her.

Their questions always gave me food for thought, they were so sweet, simple, and straightforward. Children, with their humility and detachment, teach us to raise our eyes from the ground and look at everything with wonder and delight, as they do.

Later, when I returned to France, I was no sooner through the door of the computer center before they were showing me all the things they'd done in my absence — everything from press reviews to photomontages, collections of poetry, and massive charts hanging from the walls. But the thing that moved me most was a red exercise book in which every child had written down what my adventure had meant to him or her. In it, a twelve-year-old named Mustafa had written: "I have a dream of my own and now because of Maud's project I know I can make it real. *I'm going to be a mechanic!"*

If I were only allowed to keep and cherish one memory and one triumph from my life, I would want it to be that last phrase with its message of hope, written in an unsteady, hesitant hand.

I watched for the sun's first signs of failing, and an hour later it finally dropped its guard and began to droop. This moment of calm was always one of the best of the day. The air was less cloying and the wind, freshened, caressed my tense shoulders and toyed gently with my hair.

A thick curtain of clouds fell across the horizon, as if to bring the day's performance to an end. We hadn't had much of an intermission today, and the end of the play came as a great relief.

A soft red-gold shaft of light escaped from the crest of the cloud bank, like a firework ignited at the horizon. The ocean was flooded with pink, and the waves crowded westward, hungry for the last tinges of color.

The sun took a last shy bow before rolling out a straight orange path across the water. It was the path I would follow all the way to Polynesia.

There was still a long way to go, but mysterious moments like these made up for my solitude. With nothing on my back but a simple T-shirt, I sat in the after hatch with a bowl of soup. The package claimed it was made of vegetables; I savored it like the subtlest of dishes. I watched the stars flickering on one by one, in loving company with the moon. They shed a peaceful light. They may have been millions of light years from me, alone on the ocean, but right now they felt very close.

The night was unusually clear, and at length the myriad points of light seemed to shake the firmament and stir its inky blackness. I had never seen them in such profusion, cascading right to the sea surface on the horizon. There were stars of all sizes, each with its characteristic way of shining. Some glistened lustily. Others blinked like Morse code. Still others were stars to steer by, casting a lighthouse beam.

I felt Lilliputian under these millions of bright eyes and fell to thinking about the dear ones I had left behind. At ten past one, I saw a shooting star and duly made a wish, in the hope that the Great Universe was still awake to hear it.

Every time *Océor* breasted the water, she shed a shower of phosphorescence like the fairy Tinkerbell. The sea was full of plankton, which made my little craft look as if she were wallowing in starlight. Vegetable plankton (phyto-plankton) is made up of thousands of microorganisms, a mixture whose energy value was proven by Alain Bombard, a doctor and sailor, in 1952 when he performed his "voluntary shipwreck" in the South Atlantic. Out of water, plankton look like a magic brew of glowworms, some people like the taste of them, if not the smell. As far as I was concerned, there was enough dehydrated food on board, so the question of eating plankton didn't arise. They are only present on the sea's surface, where they accomplish their process of photosynthesis by absorbing mineral salts and carbon and rejecting oxygen when exposed to light. At night every stroke of my oars surrounded me with swirling, glittering diamonds.

When I awoke, the sun was up. But the sky was wrinkled with white clouds, like a sheet of crumpled paper, which would provide some respite to my sunburn. There was a touch of sea mist, too; the light was dusty. The spasmodic motion of the sea prevented me from rowing cleanly. I ran my fingers through my salt-matted hair and rubbed my tired, swollen face. I felt miserable, as soiled as a caged animal in a zoo. I hadn't been able to bathe in a week. This was one of those days when I had no wish to go on, when a comfortable bed seemed the only refuge. Finally, I rested the oars and just sat there dismally, my head in my calloused hands.

Many minutes went by before I looked up again. I felt annihilated, as if I'd been hit over the head with a sledgehammer.

Clearly, a lack of vitamins and too many difficult nights endured recently were to blame for the state I was in.

Come on, Maud. Pull yourself together before this gets any worse.

My whole body was racked with pain, screaming for attention. I had to listen to what it was telling me. I decided to take advantage of this overcast day to wash thoroughly. The weather prospects weren't very good, and the swell was back with a vengeance, but the way I was feeling I couldn't afford to wait patiently for a hypothetical flat calm.

Océor wasn't a very stable craft at the best of times, so I'd have to be especially careful. I shipped my oars and made them fast, side by side, with a piece of rope. Then I pulled a blue plastic bucket out of the port-side locker and assembled a clean towel (which would have to last for the next three weeks), a white T-shirt sealed in a plastic bag, my rusting hairbrush, shampoo, and a big sponge for *Océor*'s cockpit. The cockpit was going to be included in the general ablutions.

Taking a shower at sea is a simple matter. You pour bucketfuls of water over your head, keeping a firm hold on the boat so you don't tumble overboard. You get soap in your eyes, get blinded, and lose your towel, then find it again.

An hour later, everything was sparkling clean. *Océor* was more or less rid of her algae and both she and I were in a much better temper.

My relationship with my body, with my feminine nature, is very important to me. More and more often today, women are freely doing things and having adventures that used to — unjustly — be the sole preserve of men. And these women stay perfectly feminine.

On land, I like to wear mascara, perfume, and pretty clothes. At sea, the contrast is stark. I watch in dismay as my body alters, my shoulders expand, and my hands blister, then grow calloused. Currently I had bruises all over me, three lumps on my skull from banging it on the hatch on my way out of the cabin, acute tendinitis in my thighs, a cracked rib, and knees grazed from rubbing against the bulkhead when I was huddled inside trying to top up the ballast tanks. Washing in fresh water was out of the question. I had to dry myself with a towel covered in salt; I had only five spare T-shirts and two extra pairs of pants; and I had to sleep on a pallet that was always damp and sometimes plain sodden. Yet careful hygiene was vital, to avoid sores, boils, infections, and any other kind of cut or bruise. So I tried to be as disciplined as possible, allowing myself only a few bodily luxuries (not purely feminine ones, either) when the squalor became too much.

I had brought along a small pocket mirror, face cream, tweezers, deodorant, and two disposable razors. Silly though it seems, these humble items offered a sure way of bringing me back to myself and raising my morale at difficult moments. It was a real pleasure at sea to spend an occasional quarter of an hour sprucing myself up, applying cream to my skin, and brushing my hair. Afterward, I felt more relaxed, happier, full of new energy. Of course, my physical aches and pains were always present, but my morale was higher and I could face the sea more cheerfully.

A group of boobies, probably attracted by the doings

aboard *Océor,* were flying in circles around me. I tried to lure them closer with offerings of cereal, but they stayed out of reach.

A small white bird with a black back had kept me company for a while when I was crossing the Atlantic. He spent the daylight hours perched on my plastic bubble, arranging his plumage and scrutinizing the water around him in hopes of spotting something to eat. I watched him surreptitiously from my bunk below. During the night, he moved to a corner of the cockpit, keeping an eye out for me. Finally, he felt so secure that one morning he started trying to stop me coming out of the cabin, screeching and flying at me aggressively. As far as he was concerned, he'd taken over the boat and didn't want me around anymore. At this point, I had to show him who was boss and I chased him away several times, gently but firmly. Realizing he wasn't the master of the ship, he flew away, leaving me to continue my voyage alone.

The sky above my head was once again a uniform pale blue, not unlike a summer sky in Provence. I bent to my oars and listened to the sea's song as it rippled beneath the prow.

I went easy with my left oar to compensate for the swell surging out of the south.

Slowly but surely I was advancing westward.

8

No Certainty Under Heaven

*M*Y SIXTY-SIXTH DAY AT SEA, March 18, brought news that my backup team had landed on Papeete. That meant preparations for my arrival were about to begin, and I wanted to burst into song.

A few soft clouds on the horizon, dawn's eiderdown, lay bathed in tender pink. It was going to be another very hot day. I put a few things out to dry and fixed them securely to the roof of the cabin so they could neither fly away nor get in the way of my rowing.

In the course of the day, the sky became completely clear, taking on a hue as pale as whitewash. It was like living in a bell jar. I closed my eyes and tried to visualize the distance I still had to row. On the other side of my bubble lay the narrow door — my passage — through which *Océor* and I might just be able to pass. I saw myself timidly opening it . . . and, hearing all the hubbub of land beyond, hurriedly closing it. I took a deep breath. All that was unreal and far away. My oars rose and sank, rose and sank. The day of arrival was not yet here.

My life kept pace with the sun as usual, my desalinator continued to yield a little more water than I needed every day, building up a reserve just in case. This extra water was stored in the forward cabin, in one of the hermetic red and white plastic jerry cans.

It's always when you least expect it that bad luck strikes. Knowing this, I was extra vigilant, to be sure nothing bad happened at this late stage of the game. *Late stage* in a manner of speaking, naturally — it all depended on the scale of your map.

The team on land had let me know I was making rapid progress. This was true, but it didn't remove the disagreeable impression I had, all alone in the infinite wilderness of blue water, that this crossing was never going to end.

So I kept rowing, fighting against the continual rearguard action of aches and pains. I kept up my schedule of regular rest intervals and massage. A few days ago, the tendinitis had spread from my right thigh to a new location, in my left wrist.

Otherwise, my body was holding up on a diet of freeze-dried food, while my soul survived on a diet of tiny things — trivia, if you like, but trivia that made sense if you put it all end to end, like the strokes of my oars. Obeying the sovereign gods of wind and sea, rising above the drudgery of my daily toil, I managed one way or another to satisfy my appetite for wonder, adventure, and change.

I was pulled from my reverie by the throb of engines.

I scanned the horizon — nothing in sight. Yet the noise was approaching at incredible speed. I looked up and was promptly blinded by the sun, unable to see what was bearing down on me. Then all of a sudden there it was, coming in fast.

A helicopter!

For a moment I just stood there — then flung myself into the cabin to grab the binoculars and the short-range handset. By the time I was back in the open, the copter was right overhead, flying in tight circles around the boat.

Through my glasses, I recognized the red-and-white insignia painted on the helicopter's fuselage — a twin-hulled canoe against a setting sun. It belonged to the national marine park of Polynesia.

I wondered what on earth it was doing out here.

Then I looked again and saw the pilot holding up a board on which was written something I couldn't make out. I signaled them to come closer. There it was: the letters *VHF.*

In my excitement I'd forgotten to turn on my radio.

There was a loud crackling sound, then a man's voice.

"*Bonjour.* We're from the frigate *Prairial.* We've been hunting for you for hours, and were just about to give up. Is everything okay?"

It was surreal. Here I was on my own, completely cut off for months — and in the blink of an eye I was back with mankind. People were hovering over my head and talking to me in French.

"Er, and good morning to you, too! Happy to hear you. Everything's fine. I'll soon be with you on land."

"*Prairial* will be alongside in about twenty minutes. In the meantime, mind if we take some pictures?"

I sat down on the forward cabin roof, deafened by the roar of the giant helicopter blades and soaked by the water kicking up around me. This swift return to the modern world seemed to have telescoped the two strongest driving forces in me: my solitary harmony with nature and my overwhelming longing for human contact.

I scarcely had time to say "of course you can" before I was transfixed by fear. Two bulky shadows were flashing to and fro beneath the boat. Sharks. Highly agitated and circling *Océor* aggressively. No doubt they were disturbed by the vibrations from the helicopter blades.

I pointed them out to the pilots, who quickly moved away. I clung tightly to my little flagstaff to avoid falling overboard.

The frigate came up very quickly. *Prairial* was a military vessel, battleship gray, about 300 feet long with a crew of over ninety men and women. I had a short conversation with her captain, Commandant François Moucheboeuf, who explained that they were on their way to join Jean-

Louis Etienne at Clipperton. Knowing I was in the vicinity, they'd made a detour to see if all was well.

I thanked them warmly, touched by this act of kindness.

The frigate lowered a dinghy with ten seamen in it, all wearing immaculate whites. They came alongside to say hello and take pictures. They studied me with broad smiles and wide eyes. I grinned back, savoring this delightful encounter. I'd never been so happy in my life to see other human beings. I looked them up and down one by one, as if they were pictures in an exhibition, drawing from their questions, their astonishment, and even their awkwardness all the magic of human contact that I had been missing so much. And since it was hard to justify in a few words why exactly I was sitting here alone in a floating nutshell, in the middle of the world's largest ocean, the fact was glossed over and set aside. Instead we spoke of the Marquesas, *Prairial*'s last port of call, of the party being prepared for my arrival, of the green mountains, the simplicity of the people, the fresh fruit — mangoes, grapefruits, guavas, and melons — and the Tahitian salads I could expect there. I savored every word, every intonation, every image of that exchange, and even before it was over my head was full of the coming wild reunions, the tables loaded with delicious food, the hours I'd spend lolling under blossom-laden trees. . . .

But now the allotted time was over and we could talk no more. The commandant was calling his men back to the ship. She had to be on her way. There wasn't a moment to lose.

As soon as the dinghy was safely back under *Prairial's* wing, her entire company lined up on deck to salute me. It was a gesture of friendship that shook me to the core — proof of the ancient solidarity among seafarers.

The French navy has always supported me to the hilt. From the day I embarked from Saint-Pierre and Miquelon in 2003 to this moment on the fringe of Polynesia, the sum of nautical miles had been matched by the same number of moments of joy, helping hands extended, and messages of sincere encouragement.

As if the whole encounter had been a dream, the *Prairial* gently put about and steamed away toward the horizon.

It was a painful parting for me. I was alone again and prey to a subtler form of depression than before. The sudden human contact had been disorienting, and now I felt like a vulnerable child abruptly abandoned. The space around me seemed much more overwhelming than it had been a few hours before. I hugged myself as an act of self-protection. My very soul seemed to ache as I watched the fast-fading shape of that kindly vessel. I began to hum a Jacques Brel song.

I consoled myself — the end of the voyage was near, the Marquesas Archipelago was only about 400 miles away. But landfall had become a chimera, a symbol of everything that was unattainable and impossible, a dream that could never come true. With every oar stroke, I imagined the island's scent of *tiaré* flowers, hibiscus, and frangipani curling around me.

Later, my father spoke to me on the phone. My family already had the pictures taken by the sailors and everyone was so happy and reassured to have fresh news that the pressure on me was eased. After months of anxiety, all our hearts were a little lighter.

I looked again at the chart, which I hadn't even thought about for a couple of hours. I was aiming for a tiny point marked in ocher, west-southwest of my present position. This was the celebrated island of Hiva Oa, north of Fatu Hiva — Thor Heyerdahl's paradise island, where he lived for several years. My spirits began to rise. One more week and I'd be there! Every hundred yards I thought I saw a dense cloud on the far horizon, of the kind all mariners know is the prelude to landfall. I squinted and strained, in the hope of sighting a shadow of the tall cliffs that were the proud defenders of the place where I would soon come ashore. Yet I knew quite well that the coast was still too distant to be sighted. Ahead there was only sea and more sea, with no trace of any lingering, premonitory cloud.

In 1968, the legendary Bernard Moitessier was a few days from the finishing line of an around-the-world, nonstop, solo race, and he was leading. At that point he decided, to everyone's astonishment, that he wouldn't cross the line after all, but head back to the open sea and sail around the world a second time. In a note tossed by catapult to the bridge of a passing tanker (more economical than the satellite telephone, which anyway hadn't been invented back then), he soberly announced that he was continuing on his long voyage "because I am happy at sea, and perhaps also to save my soul."

This simple phrase reverberated through my childhood and to this day inspires me. But as far as I was concerned, unheroic though it might be, I had no intention of turning away from my own finishing line. The birds, which were beginning to appear in force around *Océor,* came to comfort me in that decision. They wheeled joyously around me, gliding across the wavetops and tumbling on the wind like autumn leaves. Snow white, angelic, graceful, the birds would guide me all the way to dry land.

But even this charming escort did not allow me to forget the sound of the sea, its mysterious depths, its power and cruelty. The ocean was as strong and impetuous as ever and it was folly to linger.

Back at my post, gripping the oar handles in my swollen hands, I attacked my task like a quarryman splitting blocks off a stone face — only in my case the blocks were whirls of seawater, which I tore away stroke after stroke, day after day. I was slowly chipping away at the impossible in quest of my freedom.

When I was little, I used to crawl about the beach for hours, sifting the sea wrack for pebble treasure polished by the sea to a greater luster than the others. When they were wet, they looked like the gems of a diadem. I collected them greedily in my little plastic bucket, later transferring them to a wooden box at the bottom of the bunk-locker in the schooner. When they lost their sheen, I washed them in seawater and they were beautiful again. Playing with those stones I learned: never let yourself think of anything as static or preordained.

Perhaps, taking stealthy advantage of my inattention, the sky had darkened. Absorbed in my dreams of land, I failed to notice the absent sun and the freshening wind, which had begun to raise a dangerous swell. The weather was changing fast, which was not good news.

Still, I kept rowing, ticking off the miles like prayer beads.

My flags were taut and snapping in the gale. I watched the waves mounting around me, their troughs deepening by the minute. The surges were running at breakneck speed, their crests foaming with rage, then breaking dully, leaving long white trails in their wake.

Océor seemed tinier and more vulnerable than ever. I took deep drafts of air into my lungs, struggling to relax. My head was exploding with a new migraine. There was a momentary glint of sunshine; the sea turned hard as glass, glowing diabolically. I just wanted to close my eyes and be somewhere else — in woodland quiet, amid birdsong and the scent of the forest.

A monstrous wave butted *Océor* full in the stern. I recoiled in terror, grabbing for the oars, the cleats, the guard rail, anything within reach. The boat heeled hideously to port. I crawled to the safety of the cabin with the wind howling about my ears. By the time I was through the hatch and had made it fast, every muscle in my body was stiff as a board.

Inside the heat was close to unbearable. I watched the seconds, minutes, and hours ticking away on my watch as it jerked and swung from the bulkhead. The roaring outside echoed deafeningly through my wooden cage. I braced myself, trembling, clinging for dear life to the rope that ran around the cabin. From time to time, I was forced to open the hatch an inch or so to let in a little air. I could feel my strength draining away. I was slowly suffocating.

The wind steadily increased in violence. The sea had gone completely mad. The Marquesas might well be nearby, but we were in desperate danger now. And to think I had imagined the worst of the voyage was over! I fought to stay focused, though shaking with terror.

All in vain. Suddenly there was an ear-splitting roar and a wave of unimaginable size and violence engulfed the boat. I flung myself at the hatch, which I had just that moment opened a trifle. Too late, the sea was already upon me. I wrestled with the latches in a paroxysm of fear. My skull crunched against the plastic dome; within seconds I was head down in total darkness. The cabin was awash with water. The boat was settling, sinking . . . I was trapped in an underwater coffin.

I was going to die.

Stunned and unable to breathe, I panicked, swallowing seawater. After that everything happened very quickly.

The ballast came into play and my own body worked as a counterweight. *Océor,* crushed by the great wave, turned back on herself. I clung stubbornly to the hatch, which I hadn't had time to close, then found myself in the air again, shuddering, but above the surface.

We had capsized.

Heart thudding, I vomited freely into the bailing can.

Next thing I knew, the space around me was thick with the stench of burning. My camera had short-circuited and was smoldering under the duvet. I ripped out the red hot battery and tossed it through the hatch.

Then I took a deep breath, swallowed, and took stock. My cracked rib was hurting badly.

Pull yourself together.

Although the cabin was totally devastated, I noticed the red clown's nose still hanging in its place over the gallery.

The storm was continuing unabated, and I had to set about solving my problems, one by one. I started counting off tasks in order of priority. First, fetch a bucket to bail out the water. Second, remove all wet clothes. Third, the satellite phone had taken a bath and was bound to be out of commission. It needed to be put in a safe place immediately.

I made a note of everything that had been broken or damaged and carefully planned my next moves.

The interior damage was severe. The water had penetrated virtually everything. Many of the storage lockers had proved to be less than waterproof. My books were sodden, and the tiny kitchen burner was out of action. Luckily, I had a spare in the forward cabin, but I'd have to wait for the wind to die down before I could get at it. The photos on the ceiling had come unstuck and were floating in the filthy seawater sloshing around me. My dry clothes, bedcover, and mattress were all soaked. The water blasting through the hatch had stolen the last few traces of comfort left to me. The cabin had become a hostile place, and at that moment the distance I still had to travel seemed truly unbridgeable.

Two hours later saw me still crouched on my waterlogged mattress, soaking wet, exhausted, and trying to coax my phone back to life, drying it with Q-tip after Q-tip.

I thought of my family, to whom I had spoken only an hour before this disaster, blithely telling them I was okay. What would they think if I failed to reestablish contact?

Without the phone, I had no way of letting them know I was still alive. Horror of horrors, they might send the lifeboats out!

I gritted my teeth. Trembling, I reunited the handset with its battery. Nothing.

I slumped back on the wet mattress, demoralized, while *Océor* continued her struggle against the waves, tossing me pitifully from side to side with every lurch.

I remembered the surprise arrival of a major weather depression in the North Atlantic. In scarcely an hour the waves' troughs had increased in depth from thirteen feet to more than thirty. The night was inky black, snaked by flashes of lightning. The storm lasted forty-eight hours — during twenty-four of which I capsized a total of seventeen times. My sliding seat was ripped off by the waves, the flags were reduced to ribbons, and all the lights pulverized.

I spent every minute of that time praying, talking to myself to keep up my spirits, thinking of my dear ones at home, waiting by the telephone for news. When I finally crawled out of the cabin, I felt as if I'd aged ten years in that single night of horror. Sunlight had a different quality for me. I was reborn. I had been given a second life, to be consumed without restraint. I hope I have been worthy of the privilege.

With luck this time around my trials wouldn't last forty-eight hours.

I prayed reverently to the god of the sea, who I imagined was punishing my arrogance in coming to the Southern Hemisphere. And then, for the umpteenth time, I pressed the *On/Off* button on the satellite phone and was rewarded with a faint beep.

A sweet effervescence overwhelmed me. It was working. The screen was still black, but that tiny muffled sound was all the miracle I needed.

Half an hour later I carefully punched in the codes I had memorized, followed by the telephone number at home.

"..."

"Is that you, Minou?"

And then the sobs I had been holding back burst forth at last. The tears washed my eyes clear and soothed my heart. The only words I could utter were simple, reassuring, and as constructive as possible. I still had a storm to deal with.

The remainder of the night was heart-pounding. *Océor* was tossed ceaselessly by giant waves. The swell heaved on, unrelenting. I was bruised and battered all over, haunted by the dread of capsizing a second time. There was no hope of drying anything till the gale died down, and I could only hunker down, obey the rules, and wait.

At last, at four in the afternoon next day, I judged the sea calm enough to emerge from my hole and retrieve some warm dry clothes from the forward cabin. The fresh air brought me gently back to life. Standing up straight to face the sea for the first time in many hours, I surveyed my brave little boat and murmured my thanks.

The second thing I did was look for something to eat — a packet of freeze-dried couscous, which I rehydrated and wolfed down. At that moment it was the most delicious couscous on the planet.

This raised my spirits, and I called the team on shore to agree on a code, in case I ran into serious trouble. The phone would only function once in every ten attempts, so we worked out a procedure to follow if it went altogether dead. In that event, I would go outside and connect my emergency Argos light. And after that, we'd all meet on the beach.

The ocean was still in no mood for a truce, and there was no chance of getting anything in the cabin dry. I was surrounded by the noisome odors of salt, confined space, damp, and mold, and in addition I was scared, cold, and near fainting from fatigue.

Despite all that, whatever the pain and anguish I was enduring, I had to keep *Océor* moving as fast as possible, to avoid further accident and bring the crossing to an early end. I had to transform my body into a rigorous, obedient machine, allowing myself no weakness or vulnerability. I had only one objective now, and that was to arrive safely.

9

Journey's End

"YANKEE DELTA. Yankee Delta calling *Océor, Océor.* Do you read me? Over."

Yesterday, the admiral had warned me that a Guardian jet aircraft from the fleet's air division would be carrying out a surveillance flight over the zone where I was located. I eagerly awaited this event, happy to have a visitor. The only drawback was, in view of my impending arrival, I'd planned to give myself a good cleansing, and I was worried I'd be caught with soap in my eyes when the plane turned up. But I was sure they'd have a few problems locating me, so I went ahead and carried out my acrobatic ablutions as quickly as possible.

The plane's crew had picked up my latest position from Argos. I was still a microscopic speck on the vast ocean surface, very hard to see in the swells.

"Yankee Delta, Yankee Delta calling *Océor, Océor.* Are you receiving us? Over."

As soon as I heard their engines, I scrambled below to switch on the VHF. No luck. The crew made three passes, but still couldn't see me. At the speed they were going, I guessed the copilot would find it pretty hard to locate the tiny red dot of my signal flare.

"*Océor, Océor* to Yankee Delta, Yankee Delta. Do you read me? Over."

They weren't reading me because the range of my portable VHF was too short. They were scarcely in sight before they were overhead and gone again, and I was left talking into thin air.

It was depressing to watch them flash to and fro to no purpose, in and out of the clouds. I waved my arms, watching helplessly and waiting for them to make another pass. Twenty minutes went by before they were able to pick up my transmission and obtain my latitude and longitude.

"*Océor, Océor* to Yankee Delta, Yankee Delta. Position: 9° 39' 39" S and 137° 07' 08" W. Over."

The reception was patchy, and I had to repeat it about ten times before they could register the position and swoop down to join me.

Finally! The plane banked steeply and dived in my direction, like a kamikaze flying out of the sun. I ducked my head instinctively and when I looked up the plane was already climbing steeply into the sky. I gave a friendly wave and a grin I'm not sure they could see.

Mission accomplished, Yankee Delta made a couple

more deafening passes and raced away west-southwest to Tahiti.

"They're waiting for you at Hiva Oa!" was their final salute.

I had the heady sensation that I was near the coast. I lowered my oar blades and shut my eyes. The sweet scent of land, of bougainvillea flowers, already seemed to surround me.

If all went well, I would make landfall tomorrow, or the day after tomorrow at the latest. Land couldn't stay hidden for much longer. If I stuck to my guns, sooner or later it would appear on the horizon.

Those final hours were the ultimate test of my perseverance, the final battle I had to win against my own weakness.

The day seemed interminable. Patchamama, goddess of land, tortured me incessantly. The last miles were endless labor. During the night, I imagined Penelope, wife of Ulysses, creeping by to unravel the nautical miles I had accumulated in the past hours, just as she did her embroidery while she waited for her husband to come home. I spoke to the team on shore several times. A welcome was being prepared, the whole island was in a fever of excitement, everybody wanted to know when I was scheduled to arrive.

The very question irritated me. I didn't know when I'd arrive. I wasn't a sailboat or a motorboat, and my calculations were bound to be vague.

And it was hot, very hot. Nobody seemed to realize

that I, too, was fed up and desperate to reach harbor, and meanwhile I was slowly roasting on a giant grill. The people on shore had trees, roofs, fresh water. . . .

Scores of birds were dancing around me. I cast them questioning looks: Where was the land? The only answers they gave were mewings and shrill cries and incomprehensible movements. A few clouds nudged each other on the horizon. "What's the hurry?" they seemed to say.

Well, the Marquesans were waiting for me, that's what!

I kept on rowing through the long, long day. A small six-seater plane assigned to High Commissioner Michel Mathieu flew overhead. I believed it contained my family, accompanied by Raymond Gauvain, chef de bureau at the Defense Ministry. They must have been wild with impatience. I waved and watched till they were out of sight, then started thinking of all the things I would rush to do as soon as I set foot on land. First of all, a shower. . . . No, a hot bath. Then a huge meal . . . or perhaps a meal, then a swim, then a good long sleep — one exceeding sixty minutes for the first time in ages! I would pass out cold, with no need to wake up and face danger, or to bunch myself up into a ball to avoid banging myself. I would lower the shutters in the knowledge that I was running no risk whatsoever. And I'd be able to count on other people again, and not be alone anymore. . . .

For the hundredth time that day, I glanced over my shoulder . . . and saw it.

Land!

Emotion welled in my throat. Far ahead — but within rowing distance at last — was a faint pencil line on the horizon. It was blurred behind a white veil of condensation — perhaps it was a mirage . . . ? I turned away, rubbed my eyes, and looked again. No question now. It really *was* land. I felt a huge grin spread slowly over my face, till it stretched from ear to ear. I felt like a child on the night before Christmas, bursting with impatience to see this faraway bluish smudge, gradually, magically detaching itself from the rim of the sky.

That sunset was my last at sea — on this voyage at least — and it was a voluptuous performance. Everything was drenched in red and orange light, and my golden destination lay newborn before me. A few hours earlier, nothing had lain ahead but the infinite Pacific. I kept looking over my shoulder, devouring this miraculous, pink-haloed island. *Océor,* too, was bathed in color, shining crimson just like me. The moon was full, as it was on the day of my arrival from the North Atlantic. Magic enveloped me. I could already see the tops of the coconut trees and the roofs of the little houses I imagined on the island. Softly, Hiva Oa rose from the sea.

Now I was protected by a whole raft of stars, inviting me to relax and enjoy to the full these last moments of serenity and peace. Very soon I would be worlds away from them.

I inhaled a deep draft of the salt air, which for me is

the elixir of life. A dozen or so oar swirls stretched away astern, blending with *Océor's* silvery wake.

A French navy vessel, the *Tapageuse,* now arrived to escort me. Captain Yann le Roux and his crew were able to locate *Océor* thanks to her lights, which were flashing white at a much more regular rate than my excited heartbeat.

They lowered a little Zodiac launch, which raced across and came alongside. Chris and my younger brother Roch were aboard. I wanted to throw myself into their arms. The sea, which was choppy, made maneuvering difficult, and the rubber launch bumped several times against *Océor's* hull. I could just distinguish the boys' broad grins in the moonlight.

Roch, down to earth and technical as always, asked me if the ballast tanks were full. In my family, we spurn sentimentality. But I saw his clear blue eyes and in them a mix of pride and pleasure. The simple fact that he was here, squatting on a wave-tossed Zodiac in the middle of the night, defying seasickness with a face that shone with joy, told me everything I needed to know. Deeply moved, I offered him a cheek whose blush was veiled by the night. The rest of the Zodiac's crew stayed silent.

I think it was the most beautiful night of my life — that simple moment set a term to the months of solitude I had endured. We exchanged a few short words. Our hearts were too full to do any more. Chris's eyes were fixed on me, so intense that I dared not raise my own. Only the thinnest of silken threads held me in check, preventing me from breaking down altogether.

But there were still many miles to go and I made myself concentrate on Captain Le Roux's instructions. He indicated the course I should take to the mouth of the harbor. I filled my lungs with air and felt new strength flooding through me; I felt as light as a butterfly. The Zodiac sheered off and I returned to the rhythm of my oars, which suddenly seemed much easier to handle.

I still had a good eight hours of rowing ahead. The patient *Tapageuse* rode level with me across the water, constantly in view, making me feel safe at last. I was no longer alone. Hour after hour, singing to myself to stay awake, I prepared for my return to land, with all its sweetness and all its constraints. I was heading back to what we call normal life.

Why *normal*?

Normality, conformity, obedience to the rules — are these not the very things that make existence colorless? Why is it that when I come back from an adventure life seems so ordinary?

Happiness can be found in many things that are much closer to us than we imagine. It lies in doing the things we have chosen to do, in learning to do them better and better until we find in perfection true well-being. The hardest part is accepting what you are and finding the courage to make your dreams come true, along with your choices and projects. It doesn't matter if they're easy or difficult to accomplish. They can be carried out on land or sea, daily, or only occasionally. Difficulty should not be a brake, but a challenge. Happiness is a rare thing, which must be deserved, and life swings between joy and disappointment. I know that my own perpetual yearning to go back to sea is linked to the pleasure, later on, of returning to port.

One thing is certain. Happiness doesn't wait. The sea has taught me to live every sunrise as if it were my last.

On the map, the latitude of Hiva Oa is 138° 50'. I was all but there, and yet I had the impression I was standing still, just as stuck as I was the day after leaving Peru. Now that I had something to give me my bearings, the distance I had yet to cover didn't seem any smaller. Despite the nautical miles I was steadily racking up, despite the passing hours, it felt like the island was getting no closer. I cursed the sluggishness of *Océor*, lagging like an animal crawling on its belly. I had been rowing since yesterday morning and still had a whole night to go. My hands were inflamed, my shoulders tense with effort, my back one dull ache. With every movement, my cracked rib gave me pain. *Océor* lurched against the waves like a drunk making his way down the sidewalk. I paused for a moment to catch my breath and drink a mouthful of water, which no longer had to be rationed.

Ahead in the half-darkness I could make out the jagged cliffs of the island. I thought of the people there, fast asleep in their beds, lulled by night murmurs and the whirring of cicadas, protected by their dark, towering rocks.

And then the first warm, intoxicating whiff of rich land filled my nostrils.

I knew at that moment what the early explorers felt when they at last saw what they had come to find after months and years at sea. A new, virgin world. The southern Marquesas Islands were discovered by the Spanish navigator Alvaro de Mendana, who named them in honor of the Marquesa de Mendoza, wife of the viceroy of Peru. Two centuries later, and a few years after Captain Cook, the Frenchman Etienne Marchand arrived in June 1791, after five months at sea on his ship *Le Solide*. Marchand's log records that at sunrise he sighted a tall island with numerous valleys and hillsides, clothed in the most pleasant greenery and a vigorous growth of trees. I felt as if I were discovering this land of mystery and promise all over again.

My GPS, hanging from the hatch, was permanently switched on and I was checking it every ten minutes. The coast loomed. I could hear waves breaking ahead.

Three miles to go. Then two. Then one.

It was 2:32 in the morning. *Tapageuse* and the coast guard vessel that had just joined us sounded their foghorns. The deep blasts echoed again and again through the night, announcing my victory. In my right hand I waved a blinding red signal flare.

It was all over! I had done it!

In that instant, my mind flashed back to the days immediately before my departure from Callao. I saw myself full of anxiety, hiding it from the journalists, listening to the unconcealed doubts and questionings of the Peruvian naval commander. Of course, I had had second thoughts — serious ones. Success is such a fickle thing, and doubt is ever present. Until the very last moment, when I had only a few miles to row, I was preparing to hear people say, "We told you so," or "In any case, the project was impossible," and even, "No woman could ever do that."

But I had done it.

Never in my wildest dreams had I expected such a welcome. I had entered paradise and the Marquesans who lived there took me to their hearts in the most wonderful way.

Océor arrived proudly at the harbor mouth, puffing out her chest amid a swarm of traditional *va'as* festooned in her honor with bright, richly scented flowers. A traditional outrigger, specially restored for the occasion, came out to meet us loaded with virile, heavily tattooed, brown-skinned dancers, whose long hair was cinched with palm leaves. My final oar strokes were timed to the insistent beat of their music. The entire population was on the beach to greet me — several hundred people, all of whom had risen well before dawn. I drank in the odor of humankind, of trees, of land. The turquoise shallows were alive with coral and multicolored fish. At long last, I could see at close quarters the majestic isle toward which I had been progressing since January. Everything around me seemed original, in a landscape wild, poetic, and mysterious. Although my eyes stung with fatigue, the exaltation of being here kept me awake. I didn't want to miss a minute of the spectacle.

After seventy-three days of unbroken solitude, I had my reward — the realization of my dream.

A pair of muscular Polynesians came wading through the limpid water to carry me ashore. I felt awkward in their arms, but indescribably relieved that it was all over. They bore me through the waiting crowd — a sea of big black shiny eyes — and there was my mother, alight with joy and relief, waiting to wrap me in her arms. I smelled her sweet *eau de parfum* that I knew so well. I closed my eyes at the touch of her soft lips on my cheeks, so desiccated by wind, sun, and salt.

After that, everything happened in a blur, at many times the speed I was used to at sea. It was as if an hourglass had been set in motion and every grain of sand held an event. Shouts of joy, flashing smiles — my eyes hardly had time to take it all in. Before I knew it, I was surrounded by the inhabitants of Hiva Oa, greeted by Mayor Guy Ranzy and various representatives of the government of Polynesia, then deposited on a plaque set into a big stone on the beach that had my name on it.

My head spun. Loaded with magnificent necklaces and heavy diadems of *tiaré* and hibiscus flowers, I was hugged again and again by dancers, men and women, children and rowers. I was rechristened *Tahia hee tai miini o vevau nui* (Princess who dances on the waves), then made to listen attentively to the legend that came with my new name. It had once belonged to a king's favorite daughter, a princess who sailed away to discover what lay beyond the horizon. It was said that beyond that line there was a great abyss, and in it was the place of origin of the people of the Marquesas. The princess went in search of that place, but finding no end to the sea beyond the horizon, continued to sail forever across the wild Pacific.

My miseries and problems of the last few days were forgotten and I let myself be whirled along on the tide of warmth and friendship. The sun had just risen. I was exultant, reunited with the people I loved, amid the green mountains and luxuriant vegetation I had been dreaming of for three long months.

Finally, I rose from my throne to go to the island's only hotel, where my first breakfast on land awaited me. But I went nowhere. Instead I sank abruptly down again. My body was no longer accustomed to walking or even standing up. My legs had buckled beneath me from exhaustion.

Roch leaped forward to support me.

The days that followed were painful, but after doing a few exercises I readapted to life on land, which had plenty of other surprises in store for me. My first glass of fresh orange juice, for example. A fresh, homemade yogurt. Fresh pineapple . . . pure bliss. I savored every mouthful, chewing slowly and voluptuously. At last I could enjoy food that had integrity.

I fell asleep in the middle of the press conference. Only one day had been allotted to Hiva Oa and the program was a heavy one. I managed to totter through it, with Chris helping me to walk and keeping me from hurting myself.

I was taken on a motor tour of the island. It was harsh and grandiose, as paradises tend to be, a place where the fierce cannibal warriors of former times had metamorphosed into peaceful, hospitable fishermen. We drove with the car windows opened wide and I relished the warm wind in my face and hair as the landscape flew by, although the speed was frightening.

Why are we always in such a hurry? I thought of *Océor,* now all alone and moored to a buoy. I saw myself laboring at the oars. Meanwhile, everything around me seemed to be moving at breakneck speed.

I concentrated as hard as I could on the history of the island that the tour guide related, the words making their impression, but the images around me flitting away too quickly. We arrived at the village where Gauguin once lived, from which a humble pathway led to the cliff cemetery where he and Jacques Brel lie buried.

The cemetery, overlooking the Pacific, was sheltered not only by the cliffs but also by scores of palm trees, coconut trees, blossoming frangipanis, wild hibiscus with fragile yellow flowers, ylang-ylangs, and papaya trees. Vanilla vines wrapped around the trunks of mango trees, and their ripe heavy fruit lay on the ground beneath them. The air was cool. Birdsong and the soft rustle of leaves lifted by the wind were the only sounds that broke the silence. I felt completely at peace, caressed by the warmth of my hosts and soothed by nature's quietude.

Paul Gauguin's simple grave faces the sea. At its head is a replica of a bronze sculpture that the artist called *Oriri* (*The Savage*), which symbolizes the values he came to find in the Marquesas. I was deeply moved. In this enchanted place lies a man who came to Polynesia to escape the artifice and conventionality of European society. That day I understood why Gauguin spent his last years in this land. His work grew more powerful here, under the dual influences of Polynesian culture and the tropical environment. His most beautiful paintings and his masterpiece *D'ou venons-nous? Qui sommes-nous? Ou allons-nous?* (Where do we come from? Who are we? Where are we going?) were completed on this tiny Pacific island, where his life came to an end on May 9, 1903. To this day nothing disturbs his resting place among the trees.

Farther on, a stele in honor of Jacques Brel stands on a promontory where the singer once planned to build his house. Brel owned a twin-engine plane, and he used it to help out the island's inhabitants when they needed ferrying to and from Tahiti. Today, the plane has been restored and can be seen in the Atuona museum. On his tomb of gray stone are the words of his famous song, *Les Marquises:*

Veux-tu que je te dise
Gémir n'est pas de mise
. . . aux iles Marquises.

Let me tell you
Let me say
'Tis not allowed to moan or groan
. . . here in the Marquesas

Reading these lines, I was consumed by the energy flowing from this land of men. I wanted to sit down and linger awhile. I wanted to retreat for a moment to my own private world.

The ocean wasn't far away. I don't know why a vivid image came to me then, of giant manta rays slipping along just beneath its surface, showing their silvery undersides in a dance of love.

I was scarcely conscious of the ride back to the hotel. All I know is, I managed to cover the last few yards to my bed, where I collapsed and fell into a deep, deep sleep.

It was like emerging from a deep coma, a little death, when I awoke with a start fourteen hours later.

I was sorry to leave Hiva Oa, sorry I couldn't stay longer. The plane was already waiting for us at the airport, which was about the size of a village railway station in France. Still uncertain of my land legs, I followed the pilots onto the tarmac. *Océor* would be loaded into a container within the next few days and shipped back to France. My friend Thomas would stay on the island for another week to take care of the details.

Standing in the misty sunlight, I thought back on the welcome given to me the day before by the teenage girls at College Sainte-Anne, who had tracked my voyage from beginning to end. After I answered the questions they had been burning to ask me, they put on a demonstration of the *tamouré*, the local dance. With laughing faces and graceful movements, wearing matching *pareos* knotted at the hip and garlands of flowers in their jet black hair, they chanted the legends of their country to the insistent rhythm of a drum.

It was time to leave. For the final time I embraced the people who had made my arrival on Hiva Oa one of the most magical moments of my life.

A mist hung over the island, a sign, I was told, that I would return. I crossed my fingers, hoping it would be true.

We flew over Tuamotu, a scattering of atolls sheltered by a barrier of coral. There was a brief twenty-minute re-fueling halt at Takaroa, where the islanders awaited with garlands of flowers to hang around our necks. They showed us their tiny island, too, which is famous for its black cultured pearls. Before we climbed back on the plane, we were given fresh coconut milk, which we drank straight from the green husk. The soft white coconut flesh was delicious.

My stay on Papeete was also brief, with scarcely two days to relax. Again I was greeted royally by children and local authorities alike and given another new name — *Te tamia o te ra* (Daughter of the Sun).

The president of Polynesia, Oscar Temaru, invited me and my party to a banquet, where I was introduced to Tavae, a fisherman who had survived a hundred days adrift between the islands of southern Tahiti when his boat engine broke down. After the rescue operations were called off, he managed to keep himself alive on a diet of rainwater and fish. Tavae spoke no French, so M. Temaru acted as his interpreter while we feasted on flying fish that the two men had caught for us themselves the day before.

By now I was recovered, light of heart and soul, and enjoying each wonderful moment to the fullest, knowing it would all be over soon enough. I was happy, serene, eager to meet new people, to talk and share my experience. I was hungry for all the things I had missed and as impatient as a child to learn new things. From my time at sea, I had drawn new strength and, above all, a kind of stillness and serenity — which I pray will never leave me.

I wanted that time to go on forever, but already Paris was calling, and I had to obey.

It was 8:30 A.M. when I arrived at Charles de Gaulle Airport, Terminal A, on Air Tahiti flight TN22.

My story ends in the arms of my father, Marc, who had been unable to fly out to the Marquesas. I sighted him standing diffidently aside from the welcoming committee at the airport, discreet as ever, waiting patiently for me to come to him. He looked straight into my eyes, and read there that I hadn't changed. Which was all he needed to know. Life is like the sea, ceaselessly rubbing and polishing our exterior, while our inner selves remain unaltered.

"*Ça va?*" You okay?

"*Oui, ça va.*" Yes, I'm fine.

All my friends and family, as well as my sponsors, had turned out in force. Even my little niece Anya was there to embrace me and play with my necklace of shells as if I'd never been away. I knew that by tomorrow all the fuss would be over. But it didn't matter.

Triumph is something that comes and goes like a puff of smoke. On the eve of your victory, you're nowhere. Then the big day comes, and suddenly you have a big gold medal around your neck. The day after that, if you have any sense, you'll quietly put that medal away in a cupboard drawer.

But the memories stay with you for as long as you live — the best ones, probably, kept warm and alive for the rainy days of the future when you don't feel like getting out of bed. The present is already past. And I can hear the future calling me already. The future is what makes me grow.

* * *

Home at last, though my heart is still with the open sea.

I stand on tiptoe to take down a book that has long been my most precious possession. It contains the seed of a new dream — and a new project.

Epilogue

I READ A STORY AS A LITTLE GIRL that made a deep impression. It was set in another galaxy, on another planet. One man there, having lost all sense of reality, needs to be punished by the Great Universe. His sentence is that true happiness will be taken from him and hidden in a place where he will never find it again.

The Great Universe assembles a council to decide on the best place to hide true happiness. The councilors propose that it be concealed at the center of the earth, at the bottom of the sea, or on another distant planet — but none of these ideas satisfy the Great Universe. Finally it decides that true happiness should be hidden within the man himself — in the one place where the Great Universe can be sure no one will ever look for it.

Only recently did the moral of this children's story became clear to me. Solitude, effort, losing my bearings, danger — in these things the sea has helped me. Indeed, I

143

believe it will always help me to find myself, to accept what I have found and thus enrich my life. By its very nature, the sea encourages me to excel, to transform my weaknesses into strengths, to overcome my fears, to go forward, to be true and real and reconciled to my own nature. It does this by making me keep everything in proportion.

I do not measure myself against the sea, but when I am confronted by it I find the true measure of myself.

I went away in search of the essential, of simplicity, of austerity. I was hungry for new things. I came back having learned how to derive wonderment from the smallest occurrences, how to put aside my protective shell, how to savor life's simplest moments as fully as its greatest joys.

Now that I am back home in Meaux and wrestling with the modern storm that is our civilized life, I have to cling tightly to the guard rail to avoid losing my way. The hands of my watch seem to be out of control, spinning faster and faster. Business meeting follows business meeting. I am caught in the grind of a relentless mechanism. The only means I have for slowing it are moments shared with my family and others, hours spent watching the fields of the Seine-et-Marne and the Loiret as they grow and ripen, and days spent bicycling in the country, smelling the scent of earth newly ploughed or drinking in the sheer delight of trees, meadows, and birds far from the noisy world's excess.

The charts of the Pacific in my office have begun to mock and challenge me anew. I hear the siren song of adventure, and I can't get it out of my head. To still my longing, I open a bound notebook in which I have copied Bernard Moitessier's call to the ocean:

> I am a citizen of the most beautiful country in the world, a country that is vast and knows no frontiers, where the laws are harsh but simple and never play you false, where life is lived for the moment. In this kingdom of boundless wind, light and peace, the only ruler is the sea.

A wind blows through my dreams, and it carries the tang of salt. I yearn for the smell of the open sea. I am drunk with the desire for another voyage. It's my instinct — why wait? The globe on the chimney sill draws my eye like a magnet. I need to take my own course across the oceans of the world, in search of my own truth. I will do it under sail, this time — sailing was always my first love. And now the goal of a return to the sea's austerity, which has already given and taught me so much, has once again become the driving force of my terrestrial existence.

Afterword
by Michel Polacco

MAUD IS A YOUNG WOMAN OF TWENTY-EIGHT, whose surname echoes that of a great French victory — the Battle of Fontenoy in 1745, won by the troops of Louis XV commanded by the Maréchal de Saxe, against the English army of the Duke of Cumberland.

Maud's own victory has been twofold, against solitude and an environment that was often hostile. She has been able to subdue them both. After her crossing of the North Atlantic in 2003, which cost her 120 days of suffering, she turned to the Pacific. In this she was again encouraged by Gérard D'Aboville, supported by France Info — despite my own misgivings — and fortified by her reading of the work of the late, lamented Alain Bombard.

Every time we spoke on the telephone, Maud impressed me with her singular bravery — especially when I knew she was in situations so desperate that it felt as if I had collaborated in a suicide by failing to stop her running into exactly the dangers I had assumed would occur.

She acquired plenty of experience during her Atlantic crossing, and this experience was highly useful when she set out to row 4,300 nautical miles from Peru to French Polynesia, embarking on January 12, 2005. It took her 73 days to row that distance; with nothing but the strength of her arms, her willpower, and her passion to overcome the doubts, pains, and capsizings that awaited her. France Info was with her from beginning to end. She knew that her progress was being closely monitored, that she was watched over on the solitary ocean, that thousands of radio listeners were rowing with her and rooting for her in their hearts. In addition to the interviews carried out by my team of radio broadcasters, I myself called her on a weekly basis. Our satellite phone conversations were set for exactly 10 P.M. each Thursday evening. Sometimes it took me up to an hour to reach *Océor,* and several times I called from the home of my eighty-nine-year-old mother, who had written to express her admiration after reading Maud's first book about the North Atlantic and had shed tears over her sufferings at sea. A tie of friendship and affection had grown up with this sincere admirer, who followed Maud's adventures as if she were her own granddaughter.

Maud's arrival at the Marquesas Islands, the land of Jacques Brel and Paul Gauguin, was a triumph of a very high order. She had shown magnificent determination and tenacity, adding these qualities to the many other beautiful things about her. So let us read her account of this latest exploit and enjoy it to the full, while we await the next project. It, too, will be followed by France Info, naturally. What will it be? Only time will tell.

Acknowledgments

Today God gave you 86,400 seconds of life. Have you used a single one of them to say "thank you"?

— William Arthur Ward

Throughout this adventure, many individuals and organizations generously, freely, enthusiastically, dynamically, and patiently gave me help, support, reassurance, and encouragement — and I thank them all from the bottom of my heart. I want to make special mention of those listed here.

My principal sponsors:

In the City of Meaux: my thanks to Jean-Francois Copé, Ange Anziani, Christian Allard, Sébastien Actale, Pierre Corbel, Lyse Hautecoeur, and all the municipal staff.

At the Caisse d'Epargne: my thanks to Charles Milhaud, Thierry Gaubert, and Martine Cochin.

At Financière Océor/Banque de Tahiti: my thanks to

Claude Cosquer, Valérie Calewaert and Véronique Itier, with a special thought for Robert Lascar, managing director of the Omnium Group.

My co-sponsors:
In French Polynesia, my thanks to Oscar Témaru, Jacqui Drollet, and the government as a whole.
At Buro+, my thanks to Roger Ortola and Carole Gradit.

My institutional sponsors:
At the Ministère d'Outremer, my thanks to Brigitte Girardin, Hélène Camouilly, Chantal Cransac, and Hubert Derache.
At the Ministère de la Jeunesse et des Sports, my thanks to Jean-François Lamour and Xavier Mallenfer.
At the Fédération Francaise d'Aviron, my thanks to Yannick le Saux and Jean-Jacques Mulot.

My technical sponsors:
Marinepool, Simrad, Maxsea, Euro 2C/Studio 122, UTB, Oldhan, Bivouac, Disneyland Paris, Le Dessinateur, Polypat, Air Tahiti Nui, Boéro, Compagnie Hydrotechnique, Isometalux, Marne & Morin, Eterna, CMA CGM, WebLemon, U-PROD, Institut Français de la Mer, Armateurs de France, Mercator, Technologie Marine, Lestra — I thank you all.

ACKNOWLEDGMENTS

My media sponsors:

France Info, my thanks to Michel Polacco, Claudine Salmon, and Christian Bex; RFO, my thanks to Fred Ayangma and Stéphane Bijoux; 77FM, my thanks to Richard Jabeneau.

I also express my gratitude to Jean-Philippe Lemaire at France 3 Ile-de-France; to Bruce and Stéphanie de la Matinale at Canal+ and Alain and Olivier of Les Grandes Gueules at RMC. A kiss, too, to Pierre-Louis Castelli and Laurent Gauriat.

Special thanks are due to all the people who helped me with my preparation, notably:

Gérard D'Aboville, Jean-Luc Van den Heede, Jean-Pierre Evenno, Marcel Mochet, Gilles Eschallier, Jean-Paul Balcou, Patrick Filleux, Charly/Philippe/Stéphane and Jean-Louis, the *chouchous* of *Océor,* F. X. Taillefer, the Hotel Pierre, and Vacances de Port-Bourgenay, Pierre Cazeaubon, Valerie Fourrier, Stephane Dugast, Guy Vassel, Francis Valat, Sylvain Cordeau, Laurent Bignolas, Laurent Cabrol, and Isabelle Brulier.

In Lima and Callao: Pascal, Elizabeth, and Robin Charrier, the Regata Club and the Callao yacht club, Johnny Schuller, Mario Suito, and the Peruvian navy.

At journey's end: Gilles Terry, Germain Treille, Christian Durocher, the Rotary and Rotaract of Papeete, David Nataf, the staff of MRCC of Papeete, Yann Le Roux, le Pacha, and all the crew of the *Tapageuse,* Commandant

François Moucheboeuf of the *Prairial* and his crew, High Commissioner Michel Mathieu, the two pilots Jean-Luc and Jean-Luc, Guy Rauzy, mayor of Hiva Oa, and all the other Marquesans who gave me such a warm welcome; Raymond Gauvain, Luc Ankri, administrator of the Marquesas, Capitaine de Gendarmerie Jean-Marc Semenou and his adjutant Gilles Jago, Gaby, Bruno Scourzic, Gerard Bourgogne and his wife, and Raymond Graffe, *le grand prêtre.*

Heartfelt thanks, also, to my loyal supporters on land: the irreplaceable Chantal, Marc as ever in the background, Roch my handyman, Yann always there when I need him, my boyfriend Chris directing the Web site, Gipsy taking care of the children, Aude Justine my lovely nurse, Julia Huvé, Anne Massot my peerless press attaché, Thomas Bez always at my side, Frank with his bright ideas, Laurent Célarié the cameraman, Yannick Perrigot the sound man, Luc Trullemans the weatherman, Jean-Christophe l'Espagnol the photographer, and the ever-welcoming Restaurant L'Ile.

Thanks also to all my little adventurers, children of France or Polynesia as well as Belgium and Saint-Pierre and Miquelon — for their support, their penetrating questions, and their marvelous drawings, which decorated the inside of my boat.

And I take off my hat to Madam Busson, a fairy-tale schoolteacher.

My deepest gratitude goes out to my friends at the Hopital Avicenne and to Nicole Delépine and all her staff.

ACKNOWLEDGMENTS

And for having once again given me the chance to write, a big thank you to Nicole Lattes, Sylvie Delassus, and Pauline Guena.

Finally, I salute Patrick Poivre d'Avor, who was the godfather of my boat and the overall talisman of this adventure.